INVESTING IN (.

The AB

(Direct Partic

The state

and why you need to

learn about this now

iUniverse, Inc.
New York   Bloomington

Investing in Oil and Gas
The state of oil & gas, and why you need to consider this investment NOW.

iUniverse books may be ordered through booksellers or by contacting:

iUniverse
1663 Liberty Drive
Bloomington, IN 47403
www.iuniverse.com
1-800-Authors (1-800-288-4677)

ISBN: 978-0-595-53192-9 (pbk)
ISBN: 978-0-595-63250-3 (ebk)

Printed in the United States of America

Author of
Effortless Cash Flow: the ABCs of TICs
(Tenant in Common Investments)

Contents

ACKNOWLEDGEMENTS

Deep thanks go to the U.S. Energy Information Administration (EIA) for their wealth of data and information on the energy industry. Their helpfulness is and has been appreciated. I will refer to them most often as EIA throughout the book. Thanks also to the expertise and data provided by WTRG Economics and James Williams, who has not only excellent depth of knowledge and was gracious with his time, but is able to weed through overwhelming data and present it well to mere mortals. Thanks to the Association for the Study of Peak Oil (ASPO) as well.

Thanks to various experts who have written incisive and illuminating books on various subjects of oil and gas, including *A Thousand Barrels A Second* by Peter Tertzakian, *Profit from the Peak* by Brian Hicks & Chris Nelder, *The Oil Factor* by Stephen and Donna Leeb, *The End of Oil* by Paul Roberts and almost anything written by Daniel Yergin, Pulitzer Prize winner and head of Cambridge Energy Research Associates (CERA). A list of suggested reading is found at the end of the book.

Numerous experts in the oil industry and those personally known to me have been helpful and you all know who you are! Because of Regulation D issues, I have not named any of the offering sponsors here. Thanks to Larry Neely at Maverick Energy for his insights and for allowing several of his excellent graphics to be used. Ronald Swenson at www.oilcrisis.com is to be thanked for his insights and for allowing me to use the peak oil illustration. He has interesting information on solar vehicle developments that didn't make it into this book. Thanks also to Brad Updike, a due diligence analyst in oil & gas with Mick & Associates.

Thank you, Denny Crawford, for your comments on Chapter 7. Denny is the Texas Securities Commissioner. I would also like to thank Dale Hall, Gary Ackerman, Larry Lambert, John Tyler, Rex Bland, Daryl Templeton, Jeff Rose and Rusty Tweed at CapWest for their support. My biggest acknowledgment goes to Harlan, my patient husband.

This book represents my own opinions and not those of CapWest or any other entity.

All photos included in the book, except the author photo, are from iStock.com

INTRODUCTION

The purpose of this book is to help the investor decide if they should consider a direct investment in oil and gas to potentially profit - or whether they should run the other way. There are definite pros and cons in any such investment, and there is risk but there could also be opportunity. The intent of this book is to help investors sort it all out, and to help them formulate their own decisions. The book does not take any political stance on oil and gas, nor on the debate over new drilling in Alaska or the Gulf of Mexico, nor on any related political or environmental issue, but it does frame the many issues for investor background. This book is not a technical treatise on aspects of engineering, drilling, chemistry or the science of oil and gas, though it covers the essential basics for a potential investor. There are many different kinds of books about oil & gas – political, technical, research-oriented, those about peak oil, others about Saudi Arabia and books about the coming energy crisis and alternative investments. This book touches on many of those subjects, and was written specifically to educate the accredited investor* on the ABCs of investing into private offerings.

I am a licensed securities representative who assists accredited investors on a daily basis, specializing in the areas of private direct placements and alternative investments: Tenant-in-Common (TIC) properties, which are packaged commercial real estate investments with direct ownership that throw off cash flow; oil and gas investments; notes and debentures for fixed cash flow; LLC programs and specialized funds. I have found in my practice that investors are often curious about certain investments, especially those with higher cash flows or interesting tax benefits like oil and gas, but they have a fear of the unknown and a thirst to understand. Oil and gas has been generating great interest and excitement in the last few years, and so I thought this book could be especially beneficial and timely, as we move into the most important period of oil and gas in its history.

Understanding what one is investing in, the underlying asset and the macro view is key in the decision-making process; hence, why I wrote this book and my ABC's book about TICs called *Effortless Cash Flow: the ABCs of TICs (Tenant in Common Investments)*. Understanding the macro is why I cover areas like the "State of Oil & Gas", its history and tax benefits for investors before launching into details about typical investment offerings. I emphasize that I have not come from the oil and gas industry; I am not an accountant, attorney or scientist. I advise on, educate about and sell alternative investments, and I invest in them myself. Wearing another hat, I am President of a commercial real estate firm that specializes in passive income properties. I also sit on the Board of my securities broker-dealer. I lived abroad for sixteen years; I have many interests and love of cultures, businesses, art, history, geography, languages, politics and how it all fits together. Oil & gas is a piece of the puzzle.

For this book, I have conferred with and in many cases quoted oil and gas experts, and have used substantiated research statistics and facts throughout. My thanks to many are in the acknowledgement section. I have also referenced a number of books about oil and gas that are well worth reading, covering various aspects of the industry.

Private oil and gas offerings are alternative investments. Alternative investments can be defined as any type of investment outside of the traditional stocks and bonds that bring above average returns, and they are not always tradable securities. This could be anything like tax lien certificates, gold, venture capital projects, Tenant-in-Common investments, or oil & gas programs. There is a whole class of alternative investments that many savvy investors have used over the years to help build their wealth, called Direct Participation Programs (DPPs). (I address DPPs in chapter one). According to the "*Oil & Gas Financial*

Journal", more than $696 million was invested into private placement drilling programs in 2005, and it is growing each year. The Investment Program Association (IPA) reports that DPPs in 2007 surpassed the $10.7 billion record level set in 1987. Non-traded REITs are a big part of that number, but programs such as oil and gas are included and growing.

I have been investing in oil and gas deals as well as selling them for some time, and have become comfortable with the programs, the tax benefits, and the caveats. I set out to write a book focused on investing. I am a reasonably well-educated person and am aware of the general news, economics, politics and issues of the day. However, as I was writing and researching for this book, certain truths started to hit me over the head (including what we can expect over the next few decades and the dire situation ahead related to oil). Why was I not more aware and why aren't most Americans aware of the details and implications? Unfortunately, many believe that oil is abundant. Some may know it is a depleting asset but many think we will have plenty of oil for hundreds of years to come even if it is coming from the Middle East or elsewhere. Anyone who says otherwise, the popular notion goes, must be an extremist, an alarmist or maybe a conspiracy nut, or perhaps has a hidden agenda. We all know that oil is important and vital but many don't how engrained it is in our lives, in the products we depend on and how much of it is used for the very food that we eat.

During each day of the first half of 2008 as I dug into the research and as I was writing and discovering facts that were right under my nose, the price of oil and gas kept rising to new and unheard of heights, and I felt that I was in the midst of a confluence of events that were unfolding, and that we as a people are not ready for it. Many of us are in denial, sleepwalking or just focused on our own little worlds without realizing what is going on. **These are mostly events that can be of benefit to an oil and gas investor**, but are not pretty for the general public at large nor consumers nor the world economy. Digging into the issues of peak oil, consumption levels, and how the falling U.S. dollar is, shall we say, adding more fuel to the fire, along with the state of alternative fuels and the history of oil & gas, I have tried to cover areas that are important for a potential investor to understand.

The book morphed into more than just something for a potential investor – it morphed into reporting, collecting and presenting facts that every *person* should know. If you read and absorb no other background chapter, please concentrate on the "State of Oil and Gas" and let the information soak in. Understanding the big picture couldn't be more important when it comes to oil and gas.

Many changes and various bumpy roads are ahead in energy. By the same token, I feel that now can be the right time for investors with the right profile to profit, as long as they understand where the minefields are. Please note, these opinions are mine and not those of CapWest or any other entity. Please do feel free to contact me if you have questions or comments about the book. Toll free 866-891-1031; or visit my website at www.investinoil.org.

Kathy Heshelow

* Accredited is currently defined by the Securities & Exchange Commission (SEC) in Regulation D, Rule 501. Accredited is defined as having at least One Million dollars net worth, or an annual salary of $200,000 ($300,000 with spouse) and expectation of the same in the near future. Certain Trusts require Five million dollars net worth. In addition, the investor must be deemed 'suitable'.

"An investment in knowledge always pays the best interest."
Benjamin Franklin (1706-1790)

CHAPTER 1:
WHY CONSIDER AN OIL & GAS INVESTMENT?

Is now the time to consider an investment into oil and gas? Should diversification of the investment portfolio include an oil and gas component? What are the caveats, the upsides, and the issues to understand about this industry? Can I benefit financially? Why should I consider oil and gas?

Oil and gas, which fuels 88% of all of the world's energy, is in the forefront of the news and will probably remain there for some time. Prices have risen, the demand is high and continues to rise, and the ultimate supply is finite. The world, from developing countries to industrialized countries, runs on oil and gas. The U.S. is the leading consumer, but China's demand for oil is expected to continue to increase by five to seven per cent a year. If that happens, China could surpass the United States as the world's largest consumer of oil by 2025 or earlier. [1]

In May of 2008, the Associated Press wrote, "A leading global energy monitor said Thursday it is worried that demand for oil will outstrip world supply and is preparing a landmark revision of its closely watched forecasts. The International Energy Agency is studying depletion rates at about 400 oil fields in its first-ever study of world oil supply, said chief economist Fatih Birol. 'We are entering a new world energy order,' Birol told The Associated Press...The study was prompted by concern about the volatility of world oil markets and uncertainty about supply levels." [2]

The whole issue of supply and demand is important in the oil and gas industry, and important for anyone considering an investment. Supply and demand is perhaps one of the most fundamental concepts of economics and is the backbone of a market economy. **Demand** refers to how much (quantity) of a product is desired by buyers. The quantity demanded is the amount of a product people are willing to buy at a certain price. **Supply** represents how much the market can offer. The quantity supplied refers to the amount of a certain good producers are willing or able to supply when receiving a certain price. Price, therefore, is a reflection of supply and demand.

However, as micro-economists will tell you any day, there is no simple supply number nor demand number: there is only a demand curve and a supply curve. The market for oil is somewhat unusual, because neither supply nor demand is elastic. That is to say, when a large price increase produces only a small change in demand, economists would say it would be inelastic. No matter how expensive gas is, your car cannot easily switch to another fuel and you need your car to get to work or school, so you have the demand and you pay the price. The bus and plane have scheduled routes to keep and can't just stop because fuel costs more. Vehicles can't suddenly use a different kind of fuel – it simply won't work. When winter arrives, temperatures plummet and you need to heat your home, your only option may be to pay more for heating fuel. At the same time, if the gas prices fell by half, you would not drive twice as far, or turn your thermostat up twice as high. This is an inelastic situation.

The American Petroleum Institute (API) says that there is more than just the tried-and-true laws of supply and demand at work here. Tight supplies have been aggravated by political instability, resource mismanagement and weather. The Iraq insurgency, civil unrest in Nigeria, threats in Iran and political uncertainty in Venezuela are examples, while hurricanes in the Gulf of Mexico have affected operations in both the United States and Mexico. Finally, the decline in the value of the U.S. dollar against other countries has put American consumers at a growing disadvantage. American consumers must now pay more for crude oil than countries with stronger currencies.

Most goods in our economy have substitutes or an alternative supply, as David Sandalow points out in his book "Freedom from

Oil". Meaning, if an orange crop fails and the price of orange juice goes up, we can switch to apple juice, soda, milk or water. "The U.S. transportation infrastructure is almost completely dependent on oil. Although ethanol and other biofuels play a growing role, they make up less than 4% of the liquid fuel supply… When oil prices rise, few businesses or individuals are unable to find substitutes." Mr. Sandalow further points out that we have all grown up with this lack of substitutes, as did our parents and perhaps grandparents, and we consider it normal. "But it is deeply abnormal…It damages our national security, natural world and pocketbooks. It is the most fundamental problem we face when it comes to oil." [3]

There is something else about supply and demand within the oil and gas industry itself. Everything is in short supply – people, equipment, engineering skills. Because of the contractions that came with the price drops of 1986 and 1998, there is a missing generation in the oil industry, according to the Cambridge Energy Research Associates (CERA). [4] More than half the petro-professionals are less than 10 years away from retirement. A petroleum engineer graduating this year is likely to receive a higher starting salary than an Ivy League graduate going to Wall Street. Equipment is in short supply, too. There is need and demand to drill, but not enough drilling rigs or crews. Some smaller companies are buying their own equipment, while others partner up with companies to lease equipment or else they simply wait their turn for the rigs and such, which is costly. This competition for people and equipment has driven up costs dramatically. The costs and shortages cause delays to new projects, CERA says.

The public focuses on the price at the pump, but the oil industry is preoccupied, and even somewhat stymied, by how rapidly their own costs have risen – far exceeding the rate of general inflation, says Daniel Yergin, head of the CERA. The latest IHS/CERA Upstream Capital Cost Index – the consumer price index for the oilfield – shows that costs for developing a new oil or natural gas field have more than doubled or tripled over four year period. Some costs have risen even more: a deep-water drill ship might have cost $125,000 per day to rent four years ago. Today it goes for more than $600,000 per day – if you can find one.

Prices on equipment may have stabilized or even dropped very recently, according to some data, but the relative price has increased tremendously over the last four years, as seen in this chart courtesy WTRG Economics:

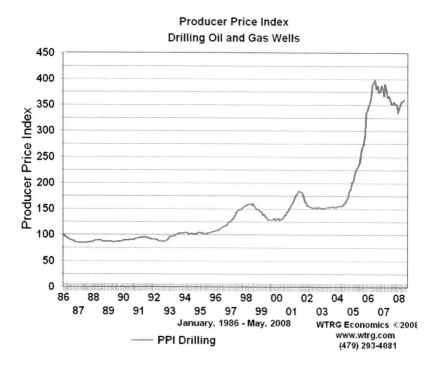

Courtesy of WTRG Economics

Oil and gas are commodities. **What is a commodity?** Commodities are simply raw materials used to create the products consumers buy, such as wheat, gold or petroleum. "Soft" commodities are those that cannot be stored for long periods of time, such as sugar or coffee. Commodities are "real assets", unlike stocks and bonds, which are "financial assets". They tend to react to changing economic fundamentals differently than traditional financial assets. Commodities have evolved as an asset class unto themselves with the development of commodity futures indexes. There are several reasons that investors may choose a commodity; first, as an asset class, they have outperformed traditional assets such as stocks and bonds. Over the five-year period ended March 31, 2006, the Dow Jones AIG Commodity Index has returned 10.6%, versus 2.6% for the S&P 500, according to PIMCO (Pacific Investment Management Company). [5] Commodity prices have been driven higher by a number of factors, including increased demand from China, India and other emerging countries that need oil, steel and other commodities to support manufacturing and infrastructure development. Simply put, "when unexpectedly high demand strains existing production, prices rise sharply as buyers scramble for scarce supplies." [6] According to PIMCO, economic factors are likely to support continued gains in commodity index returns. While the benefits of commodities may be substantial, the asset class entails risks as well. Commodity returns can be about as volatile as equity returns, potentially resulting in periods of underperformance. For example, annualized monthly volatility from January 1990 through March 2006 was 12.1% for the Dow Jones-AIG Commodity Index, 13.9% for the S&P 500, and 18.8% for the Goldman Sachs Commodity Index. **Despite the similar volatility, equities and commodities have rarely fallen in the same year. This is why commodities or commodities-based investments can be a good hedge against equities in your portfolio**.

"Oil has become the 'new gold'—a financial asset in which investors seek refuge as inflation rises and the dollar weakens," said Daniel Yergin. "The credit crisis has been fueling the flight to oil and other commodities, and that will last until the dollar strengthens or the recession becomes more pronounced." [7] On the psychological level, investors see that financial institutions are struggling (Fannie Mae and Freddie Mac are in crisis, Bear Stearns collapsed, Indy Mac Bank failed at this writing), foreclosures continue while airlines and carmakers are in trouble and jobs are being lost. Investors can counterbalance some of the shell-shock and investor fatigue by diversifying into something that is rising, performing and in demand at the moment, like oil and gas.

There is no strategic national energy policy at this time. There is no meaningful support (yet) for alternative energies though there is growing interest and some exciting advances. There is no consistent national political backing or serious focus on viable energy options. Some columnists have called our true energy crisis one of timid leaders and poor leadership. "Our political dialogue about oil is stuck in the 1970's," says David Sandalow in "Freedom from Oil". [8] There are some political and private groups addressing the issues and some states are implementing incentives. There have been good, deeply-researched studies done, some presented to the powers-that-be in Washington. There are some private companies developing alternatives to help alleviate the situation, and there have been technological advances within the oil and gas industry over the last decade. However, until and unless there is focus on viable alternatives – choices of other energies to be developed to use alongside oil - the same old game will continue: the world runs on oils and gas, the world gobbles up and wants more oil and gas, and the industry continues to extract and produce it while prices rise.

Keep in mind, if an energy policy was formulated today, or a major decision were made yesterday, experts agree that it would most likely be 7 to 10 years until we would see the results. That is, if we decided that more drilling should be opened up in Alaska or the Gulf of Mexico, the entire process takes much time (and money), with results on that action seen by consumers in 7 to 10 years. By the same token, if certain alternative sources would be proposed for larger scale application and supporting infrastructure, such as wind power, nuclear or solar, it will take time depending on the source or technology for such sites to become operational. Alternatives need financial initiatives (meaningful long-term ones, not 1 or 2 year tax incentives or breaks) and support to gain more ground. The point is, until Americans and the politicians who represent them understand and decide a shift in energy is absolutely necessary, the status quo is here to stay for some time. This is an important fact for investors to know. Oil and gas isn't going anywhere soon.

Consumers feel it in their pocketbooks: whether they are filling up the gas tank of their car, paying their heating bill, or paying more for products like groceries or airline tickets which are reflecting the higher energy costs. **By the same token, investors can feel it in their portfolios! They can feel some of the daily losses offset with returns**

on investments into oil and gas. That is the first reason why investors may want to consider a direct oil and gas investment. Investing into some form of a commodity that is in great demand, and in lessening supply, is one strategy or reasoning behind the investment choice.

So why else should one consider looking at an oil and gas investment. The first reason mentioned above: the **demand** for this commodity is great and is growing, with our entrenched oil infrastructure. The second reason mentioned was that this commodity can help **hedge** against rising prices and against movements on stocks or interest rates, especially in an inflationary period.

Other reasons to consider an investment besides supply/demand and pricing are:

- **Tax benefits**. Certain investments like drilling offer excellent write-offs, put into the tax code by Congress. There are various tax benefits available to investors depending on the type of investment made, discussed in chapter 5.

- **Diversification** of the portfolio.

- **Potential Cash flow**. There is no guarantee as to the amount of cash flow and performance, but cash flow is tied to the price of oil and gas (among other things), and that trend has been high and strong (and relates to supply and demand). The cash flows of operating wells with viable sponsors are besting typical real estate deals and many (or most) other types of investments. Even if the price of oil drops, most experts don't believe there would be a major collapse in pricing. Many oil and gas offerings show proformas based on $50, $60, and $80 per barrel oil in order to be conservative, even though oil is currently at $140+ at this writing and has been above $100 since the beginning of the year.

What are two thumbnail reasons why you may not want to invest?
- **Oil and Gas are depleting assets.**
- **Risk and volatility.** I go into detail about the risks and the downsides to consider throughout the book but specifically in Chapter 8.

There are various ways to add oil and gas to your portfolio - some investors choose stocks of oil companies, others choose mutual funds or ETFs devoted to energy, some buy mineral rights to a property and wait for it to be leased and drilled, while still others may deal in the futures market or margin trading. But for qualified investors, and the subject of this book, a 'Direct Participation Program' (DPP) – which is direct ownership - can be a most favorable way invest, to gain excellent tax-write offs not available in the other choices and gain higher potential cash flows to bump up your portfolio.

What is a Direct Participation Program (DPP)?

A Direct Participation Program (DPP) is defined as a business venture or investment program designed to let investors participate directly in the cash flow and tax benefits of the underlying investment. If you buy an energy stock, you are a stockholder of the company but the actions, tax write-offs and net cash flow are all benefitted by the company itself, not the stockholders directly (you can't write off drilling costs, for instance). The energy companies typically reinvest profits back into exploration and development, effectively giving away control of your profits. In a DPP, you own a share of the actual assets of an operating company or own a percentage interest or units in the offering, with the resultant cash flow and tax benefits. So the advantage of these programs are that you get all the benefits of being an owner without having to set up a company or become an oil expert. You receive revenues, you directly deduct expenses, and you benefit from incredible tax incentives (depending on the type of program). You can even hold DPP's in your retirement account if it seems suitable.

DPPs are generally passive and relatively illiquid investments, often in real estate or energy-related offerings, and are often tax-advantaged. The pooled investment funds are used for the program's investment goals, such as drilling, extracting and then selling oil and gas for the cash flow, or acquiring producing wells or mineral rights with royalty payments. However, today many investors do not necessarily view tax strategy or tax reduction as the only advantage, as they did in the 1980's (thank goodness!). DPPs must compete with other securities and investments as to yield, rate of return, long-term performance and structure, and they must make sense as an investment on their own, rather than to just to rely on tax sheltering. This is the way it should be.

The Securities Act of 1933 defined 'securities' to include any profit sharing agreement, *investment contract* or *fractional undivided interest in oil, gas or mineral rights*. DPPs are usually private placement securities sold to accredited or sophisticated investors and are sold following the rules of Regulation D of the 1933 Securities Act.

A **Private Placement** is a security offered to a limited number of accredited investors, as defined in requirements for a Regulation D offering. Private offerings are exempt from public registration under the Securities Act of 1933 as stated in Section 3 (b) or 4 (2) of the Securities Act. (Under the Securities Act, any offer to sell securities must either be registered with the SEC or meet an exemption). In 1982, the SEC adopted Regulation D, commonly called Reg D, which set forth clearly stated rules for exemption. The private placement exemption is based on the theory that sophisticated investors with access to full information about an investment do not need the same protection afforded by public registration. The issuer is required to make extensive disclosures regarding the nature, character, and risk factors relating to an offering. A Private Placement Memorandum (PPM) or offering memorandum is the key disclosure document of the private offering.

Reg D offerings are restricted in certain ways, in addition to them being available only to accredited investors. Among other things:
* No general solicitation or advertising is allowed to market a specific private placement security. (This is why you never see advertisements about specific offerings, and why you should never receive a cold call or unsolicited fax about a private oil and gas deal.) Only generic ads or educational information can be used, or a tombstone ad after the offering is sold and full and even that is not common.

* The sponsor must be available to answer questions by prospective purchasers, and all investors must have access to meaningful, current information.

* A purchaser must acquire the security for investment, not for the purpose of further distribution or resale.

* A purchaser or buying entity must be accredited as defined in Regulation D. Most people reading this book would fall into the category of minimum $1M net worth or $200K annual salary ($300K with spouse), and expectation of same in future. Certain trusts may require a $5M net worth. The regulations are such that being accredited is only part of the puzzle – being 'suitable' is the other part. Investors must have liquidity in their portfolio (as DPPs are generally illiquid), and they must have a profile that is suitable for such an investment. The situation is discussed with your licensed securities representative when you are considering such an investment, and is addressed further in Chapter 8.

You should know that some drilling programs offer themselves direct and not in a DPP format or through securities broker-dealers, but all of the issues presented in this book and points about due diligence would apply to those programs as well.

Oil and Gas DPP or public direct deals enable the investor to invest cash into a specific offering (often structured as an LLC or LP), receive the cash flow directly from the enterprise, and take proportionate tax benefits accordingly. Once in a while, an offering may qualify for a 1031 tax deferred exchange. Investment minimums of $10,000 to $25,000 are common for many of these programs, while some require at least $100,000 including most 1031 programs. I will discuss the various and typical oil and gas programs in Chapter 6 including the due diligence that investors should consider, and summarize the pros and cons of these investments in Chapter 8.

William E. Weidner wrote in "*Oil & Gas Investor*" (January 31, 2003)," So far this decade, the oil and gas industry is attracting and receiving an outstanding share of private placement equity. Today's contrast with the 1990s is striking. Last decade, oil and gas fund returns were not high enough; today they are considered by some to be almost too high. This sea change has created a wave of fresh private equity capital available to proven management teams in the energy sector." [9]

I do not recommend that any large portion of a portfolio be invested into oil and gas. Many investment experts suggest that 10% to no more than 25% of the portfolio should be in energy. In fact, small investments are the most prudent because of the general potential volatility. An investor must have some risk tolerance. There are some choices that are more conservative and less volatile, such as royalties or structures such as debentures based on energy. Other offerings involved with drilling, working interests, reworks and the kind have higher rewards but also higher risks involved. Use of newer and better technologies, basics like where the drilling is to occur and who is in charge will have a bearing on risk. It is for the investor to determine their own tolerance, after examining, studying and grasping the various programs and the background information in this book. After understanding the issues, it is easier to decide. And that is what this book will attempt to assist with!

"He who owns the oil will own the world, for he will own the sea by means of heavy oils, the air by means of refined oils and the land by means of the petrol…And in addition to these he will rule his fellow men in an economic sense, by reason of the fantastic wealth he will derive from oil – the wonderful substance which is more sought after and more precious today than gold itself."
Henri Berenger, French industrialist, senator and diplomat. 1921

"It's no secret anymore that for every nine barrels of oil
we consume, we are only discovering one."
-The BP Statistical Review of World Energy. June 21st, 2008

CHAPTER 2:
THE STATE OF OIL AND GAS

What is the state of oil and gas? Simply put - complicated, difficult, politically-charged and even emotional. The crux of the matter is this: we and most economies and nations of the world are incredibly dependent upon oil and gas. There is less of it, or shall we say a finite reserve, but more demand each year. Our infrastructure is built around having it and using it (at a reasonable cost, we thought). Oil and gas fields are steadily declining and the cost of extraction is increasing. Oil is the lifeblood of our civilization today, and though we act as we believe otherwise, it will not last forever. And there is the matter of a great wealth transfer away from the U.S. to consider. The United States and other nations need sound energy policies that address political, economic and environmental concerns. No country is energy independent. We live in a world of energy interdependence.

As mentioned in Chapter 1, until clear policies or groundswell advances come through to work on the crisis at hand, oil and gas is dominant in the world of energy. At a Yale conference concerning the future of energy in November 2007, Daniel Esty (Yale professor and author of "Green to Gold") said, "It's a fertile moment for change"... emphasizing that Americans are eager to see a new direction in the future of energy and that long-term solutions will require bold thinking. He believes the most viable solutions to energy challenges come from the private sector, not government intervention.[1] Politicians are usually reactive to situations rather than proactive, and in fact what politician today wants to the be harbinger of bad news and possibly lose votes? It will take courage.

The word **petroleum**, from the Latin "petra" which means rock (or earth) and "oleum" which mean oil – 'rock oil' or 'oil of the earth' - generally refers to crude oil or the refined products obtained from the processing of crude oil. We find petroleum products in every area of our lives: the gas we use to fuel our cars, the heating oil to warm our homes, the propane for our outdoor grills, the fuel for our airplanes and boats. Many products we use on a daily basis are petroleum-based, or use petroleum in their production. These include medicines, plastics, computers and food items. "It is estimated that for every calorie of food we consume in the U.S., 10 calories of fossil fuel input were needed in the form of fertilizers (made from natural gas); pesticides and herbicides (made from oil); fuel to run the machines that plant, tend, harvest, transport and process the goods; and fuel to deliver them to your grocery store and keep them cold there. And that doesn't even count the energy needed to transport you to the store…nor the energy used to cook the meal." [2]

One barrel of oil has as much energy as twelve people working full-time all year, says Roscoe Bartlett, a scientist and U.S. Congressman.[3] Matthew Savinar says that one man would have to labor 25,000 hours to match the energy in one barrel of oil.[4] This kind of energy is what has expanded exponentially the world industries, abilities and economies.

Take a look at the following chart from WTRG Economics which shows U.S. petroleum consumption and pricing from 1973 to 2007 to get a perspective on our rising consumption:

Petroleum Consumption and Price

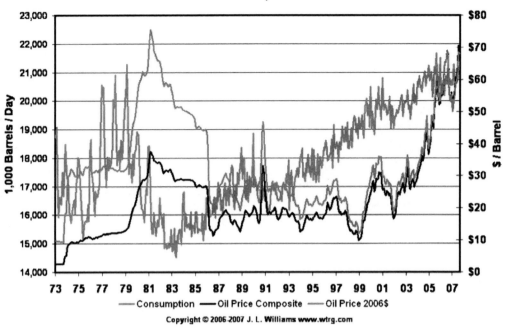

Courtesy of WTRG Economics

Annual per capita consumption in the US is 25 barrels, as opposed to Japan at 14, Britain at 11 and China at 2 (and growing). "…The world now consumes oil at the staggering rate of a thousand barrels a second" – or more now. [5] It is hard to fathom! A thousand barrels a second. The *World Energy Outlook* is produced annually by the OECD (Organization for Economic Cooperation & Development) and is an authoritative source on trends. The 2007 Outlook reports that the United States demand for oil is expected to increase 30% and natural gas by 50% over the next 20 years. However, U.S. domestic oil and gas production is declining at 4% to 6% per year. The same report says that world energy consumption is projected to increase 57% from 2004 to 2030. Total energy demand in non-westernized countries is projected to increase by 95%. [6]

U.S. Imports

The U.S. is the world's leading importer and consumer of oil, though it is also the 3rd largest producer and exporter. Some may be surprised to learn that almost 50% of our imports came from the Western Hemisphere (North, South, and Central America) in 2006. We imported only 16% of our crude oil and petroleum products from the Persian Gulf countries of Bahrain, Iraq, Kuwait, Qatar, Saudi Arabia, and United Arab Emirates. In 2007, that number was 21%, according to the Energy Information Association (EIA). We are the world's largest importer of oil, with dependency on imports at about 60% to 65% of our needs. **Concerning imports, there is an important fact to note. American dependence on oil has grown from 10% in 1970 to 65% by 2004.** Some industrialized nations like Japan and Germany have dependency levels of 90% to 100%. Our Strategic Petroleum Reserve normally holds enough oil for about a 33 day supply if all imports were cut off (it used to be closer to 60 days).

During 2006, the five largest suppliers of crude oil and petroleum products imported to the United States were:

Canada (17.2%)
Mexico (12.4%)
Saudi Arabia (10.7%)
Venezuela (10.4%)
Nigeria (8.1%)

As far as the top five importers in the first months of 2008, using EIA data, little has changed. As of May 2008 (at the time of this writing), the top five remained the same with Saudi moving up slightly ahead of Mexico, followed by Nigeria and Venezuela. The rest of the top ten sources, in order, were Iraq, Angola, Algeria, Brazil and Kuwait. Total crude oil imports averaged 9.921 million barrels per day in April of 2008, which is an increase of 0.303 million barrels per day from March 2008.

Crude Oil Imports (Top 15 Countries)
(Thousand Barrels per Day)

Country	Apr-08	Mar-08	YTD 2008	Apr-07	YTD 2007
CANADA	1,952	1,795	1,902	1,909	1,846
SAUDI ARABIA	1,453	1,535	1,519	1,458	1,358
MEXICO	1,259	1,232	1,230	1,460	1,471
NIGERIA	1,115	1,154	1,105	891	1,089
VENEZUELA	1,019	858	990	1,182	1,070
IRAQ	679	773	693	562	488
ANGOLA	579	384	469	514	556
ALGERIA	393	247	300	530	495
BRAZIL	201	188	182	175	174
KUWAIT	176	199	218	126	187
ECUADOR	160	231	203	159	200
COLOMBIA	149	135	168	79	100
CHAD	133	101	110	80	76
RUSSIA	106	108	77	269	137
LIBYA	85	75	68	45	56

Total Imports of Petroleum (Top 15 Countries)
(Thousand Barrels per Day)

Courtesy of the EIA, the top 15 countries importing to the U.S. as of June 2008.

21% of all imports to the U.S. came from the Persian Gulf in 2007, as seen from the EIA data below.

JANUARY - DECEMBER 2007
(Thousand Barrels)

	Total	Persian Gulf	% Persian Gulf
Totals:	3,628,696	768,734	21%
Company			

Courtesy EIA: Persian Gulf imports in 2007

While we are the top importer in the world, it may indeed seem surprising that we export more than 1M +/- barrels a day of petroleum products. As noted by the EIA, it turns out that exporting some barrels and replacing them with additional imports is the most economic and efficient way to meet the market's needs. For example, the Gulf Coast may export lower quality gas to Latin America while the East Coast imports higher quality gas from Europe. There are logistical, regulatory and quality considerations involved, and the EIA says that the efficiency of the markets has been increased and consumers have benefitted. In addition, the amount of crude oil produced (domestically) in the United States has been getting smaller each year while the use of products made from crude oil has been growing, making it necessary to bring more oil from other countries.

Within the U.S., the top oil-producing states are: Texas, Alaska, California, Louisiana and Oklahoma with about 25% handled offshore at this writing.

So who is producing worldwide?

The five biggest world oil producers are Saudi Arabia, Russia, the United States, Iran and China.[7]

Saudi Arabia is the largest producer and has approximately one-fifth of the world's reserves (265 B barrels +/-)

Russia is 2nd largest producer and has 60 B +/- barrels of reserves.

US is the 3rd largest producer but is producing less and importing more so is a net oil importer. We have about 21 B known barrels in reserves.

Iran is 4th largest producer and has 96 B barrels +/- or 10% of the world's reserves.

China is the 5th largest producer and sits on 18.3B +/- barrels of reserves, but like the US is a net oil importer, and has now become the world's second largest oil consumer after the US.

Note: I discuss reserves in a later chapter – not all reserves may be as reported by various countries.

A good illustration of worldwide oil follows here, courtesy of Maverick Energy:

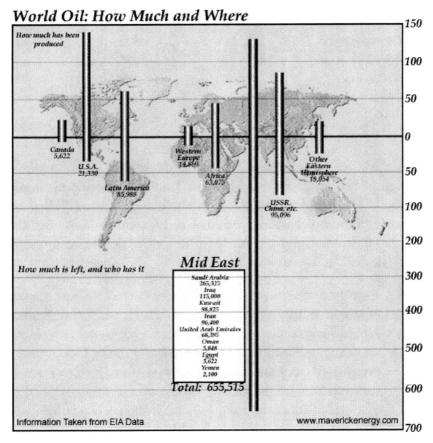

Compliments of Maverick Energy

According to statistics put together by the Wall Street Journal on June 20th, 2008, oil DEMAND PER DAY (in mil barrels) in the world, along with their stated supply is as follows:

	Demand (mil barrels)	Supply (mil barrels)
North America	24.9	14.2
Europe	15.2	4.9
Pacific	8.9	0.7
China	7.8	3.8
Other Asia	9.5	n/a
Middle East	6.7	14.1
Latin America	5.7	4.0
Former Soviet	4.1	12.8
Africa	3.1	7.0
Other	0.8	2.7

We are talking about a global product with global needs – and of course, global implications. Your own investment inside the U.S. can and will be affected by worldwide events. What are some of these global risks? Michael Brush addressed several of the geopolitical hotspots succinctly in his article "*It's time to invest for $100 Oil*", as follows: [8]

• **Iran:** Iran says it wants to produce more electricity from nuclear power so it can sell more oil abroad. But U.S. intelligence experts suspect the country is also developing nuclear weapons that could fall into the hands of terrorists. "The U.S. is pretty determined to stare 'em down," says Tom Petrie of Petrie Parkman & Co., the Denver brokerage and investment bank that specializes in the energy sector. If the confrontation boils over into military strikes on Iranian nuclear facilities, the price of oil would go bonkers. Iran could retaliate by cutting back production or closing the Strait of Hormuz, through which much of the oil from the region passes, speculates Rep. Roscoe Bartlett, R-Md., who follows energy issues closely.

- **Iraq:** Ongoing attacks by insurgents on the energy infrastructure have made it impossible for Iraq to reach its goal of producing 3 million barrels of oil a day to date.

- **Saudi Arabia:** Saudi Arabia is the largest OPEC producer and controls much of the cartel's spare capacity. But it faces threats from al-Qaida and potential terror strikes on its oil infrastructure. The country's regime also faces civil unrest. "One scary scenario is that zealots take over in Saudi Arabia because they are unhappy with the royal family," says Bartlett.

- **Nigeria:** Nigeria's rich reserves make it one of the world's top oil-producing nations. But most of Nigeria's oilfields are in the Niger Delta, a region where poverty and unemployment fuel a long-running conflict between locals and the oil companies. Attacks by rebels on the energy infrastructure have shut down about a quarter of the country's production in 2006 *(and this has continued into 2008; comment by author)*.

- **Venezuela:** Venezuela, the world's fifth-largest oil exporter, is in talks to become a major supplier to China. That would tighten supplies around the globe, since more oil would be locked up in transport during the trip to China, says Petrie. Another potential problem is Venezuela's increasing ties with countries such as Russia, which is supplying military equipment, says Holmes. If this rekindles the Monroe Doctrine and the United States takes steps to limit Russian involvement in Venezuela, that would be bad news for oil prices.

Here are two more examples of global actions that make an impact:

The Wall Street Journal reported on June 20, 2008 that "China, widely seen as the one nation most responsible for the soaring demand and price of oil in recent years, reminded the world it can nudge both in the other direction as well." China raised its base price of gas inside the country by 17%, its biggest increase in four years, and subsequently benchmark crude oil on the New York Mercantile Exchange fell $4.75 to $131.93 (a drop of 3.5%). This "is a measure of how the Asian giant is gaining game-changing market influence over a host of commodities…" The article continues, "The complexities of the Chinese energy market may confound global traders, at least in the short term. Beijing's move could raise China's demand for oil imports at first rather than tamp it down, because Chinese refiners will likely ramp up their activity and reduce energy shortages in the country, now that they can charge higher prices. That could lead to global price gains." [9]

The Associated Press reported on that same day, June 20, 2008 that militants raided oil installations off Nigeria's coast and that Royal Dutch Shell was forced to cut production. "The group is Nigeria's most effective militant gang. Its campaign of bombing pipelines and attacks on export facilities, launched in 2006, had already slashed Nigeria's daily oil output by about 20 percent, helping send global oil prices to all-time highs. Thursday's attack by gunmen trimmed that 10 percent further." [10] The next day, the Wall Street Journal reported that "Crude-oil futures rose 2%, boosted by news of supply interruptions in Nigeria and potential for rising tensions between Israel and Iran… Royal Dutch Shell declared *force majeure* on 225,000 barrels a day at its Bonga production facility off the coast of Nigeria after an attack Thursday…" [11]

OPEC (The Organization of the Petroleum Exporting Countries) is an important element as well. OPEC is a thirteen nation permanent intergovernmental organization, created at the Baghdad Conference in 1960, by Iran, Iraq, Kuwait, Saudi Arabia and Venezuela. The five Founding Members were later joined by nine other Members: Qatar, Indonesia, Libya, United Arab Emirates, Algeria, Nigeria, Ecuador (suspended its membership from December 1992-October 2007 and then reinstated) and Angola. Gabon was a member from 1975–1994. OPEC coordinates and unifies the petroleum policies of its Member Countries, who produce about 40 per cent of the world's crude oil and 15 per cent of its natural gas. However, OPEC's oil exports represent about 55 per cent of the oil traded internationally. Therefore, OPEC can have a strong influence on the oil market, and their actions – such as stepping up supply or reducing it - can affect the price of oil and gas worldwide.

A good illustration of this very point follows, from WTRG Economics:

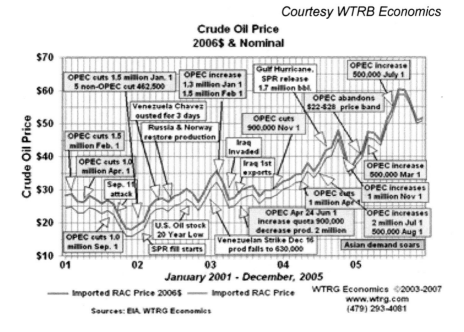

There will always be events, both big and small, on the political and world scene that will affect oil and gas, and these examples are but a taste. A basic awareness of this is important if one is going to invest in an oil and gas program.

What are other issues that can affect pricing and supply?

Infrastructure. The infrastructure for oil and gas (refining centers, pipelines, etc.) in the U.S. is aging and in some cases, in disrepair. This can affect pulling the oil or gas from the ground, refining, transporting and getting it to the consumers. In 2007, the New York Times reported that "Oil refineries across the country have been plagued by a record number of fires, power failures, leaks, spills and breakdowns… causing dozens of them to shut down temporarily or trim production.

The disruptions are helping to drive gasoline prices to highs not seen since last summer's records. These mechanical breakdowns, which one analyst likened to an "invisible hurricane," have created a bottleneck in domestic energy supplies, helping to push up gasoline prices ...A third of the country's 150 refineries have reported disruptions to their operations since the beginning of the year [2007], a record according to analysts." [12]

In fact, the Washington Post reported that "American refineries are aging and prone to accidents and other problems that require extended periods offline to remedy. No new refineries have been built in 30 years, largely because Clean Air Act regulations make building new ones prohibitively expensive, oil analysts say. Attempts by Congress to encourage new refinery construction through tax breaks and other enticements in recent years failed to produce the desired results. Most new refineries are being built in China, the Middle East and other countries where regulations are less restrictive. That has led to an increase in imports of gasoline as well as oil." [13]

According to the EIA, the U.S. had more than 300 operating refineries in the early 1980s. By 2007 the number of refineries in the U.S. had been cut in half (down to 149). From 1975 to 2000, the U.S. Environmental Protection Agency received only one permit request for a new refinery. A new refinery has not been built in the U.S. since 1976. **However**, according to the American Petroleum Institute (API) in an opposing view to press articles, U.S. refining capacity has increased by 20 percent even though there are fewer refineries. Why? Because it is more cost effective to add on to a refinery than to build a new one. The elimination of subsidies under the government price and allocation controls in 1981 led to the closure of many smaller, (sometimes) less efficient refineries throughout the 1980s and 1990s. The API data says that U.S. fuel production reached a record high in 2007 as refinery capacity expanded for the 11th straight year. U.S. crude oil production also rose in 2007, the first annual increase since 1991, according to API's year-end Monthly Statistical Report. [14]

According to the EIA, current domestic refinery expansion plans could boost domestic refining capacity by another 800,000 barrels per day by 2010, which is the equivalent of four new refineries.

Investment of as much as $88B since 1990, according to EIA, has been made in technologies to meet the stringent Clean Air Act of 1990. A number of refinery modification or expansions have been announced to handle increased processing of heavier crude oils, including oil derived from Canadian tar sands. This additional crude from Canada, a nearby source, could enhance our domestic energy supply.

What is a refinery and why is this important? It is the factory or place where crude oil is processed into petroleum products. Because many different pollutants can escape from refineries into the air, the government monitors refineries to make sure that they meet environmental standards. Crude oil contains hundreds of different types of hydrocarbons all mixed together, and there are many different types of crude oils. The different types of hydrocarbons have to be separated, using various types of technologies and processes, in order to get the useful end product. This is what oil refining is all about.

As with most aspects of the U.S. oil industry, the Gulf Coast is by far the leader in refinery capacity, according to the EIA. It has more than twice the distillation capacity as any other region in the U.S. The largest concentration of refining in the world is actually in North America, accounting for one-fourth of the crude distillation worldwide. Refining, though, has been significantly less profitable than other segments of the oil industry since the 1990's – refining margins peaked in the late 1980's. The role of the independent refiners has grown substantially, often due to refinery purchases from major companies looking to streamline or refocus the company efforts. Independents have been in a period of consolidation.

Moving on, another subject is widely discussed on every front, within the industry and outside of it, and it will not abate: **the declining supply of oil**, how much is really left and the subsequent results of this.

Hubbert's Peak or Peak Oil – what is it?

The late Dr. M. King Hubbert (1903-1989) is well known as a world authority on the estimation of energy resources. Much has been written and analyzed about Hubbert's analysis and work on peak oil. Dr. Hubbert, who worked as an assistant geologist for Amerada Petroleum for two years while pursuing his Ph.D., became a long-time Shell Oil employee and later geologist for the U.S. Geological Survey. He also held positions as a professor of geology and geophysics at Stanford University from 1963 to 1968, and as a professor at UC Berkeley from 1973 to 1976. Hubbert proposed the results of his study in 1956, which became known as Hubbert's Peak. Essentially, the bell-curve analysis indicated that our conventional crude oil production would go over the top of a great curve in 1970 and start downwards, which has actually proven true. He was initially ridiculed by some when the reports came out. However, we never produced more oil than we did in 1970. He predicted the decline would continue until reserves ran out – sometime late in the 21st century. The peak of production is passed when about half of the total has been taken. The following illustrates this, compliments of Ronald Swenson (www.oilcrisis.com)

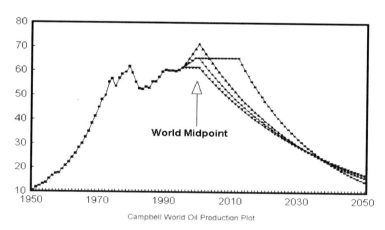

Campbell World Oil Production Plot

To clarify here, peak oil is actually a *study*, not a theory, and the top authority on peak oil is the Association for the Study of Peak Oil (ASPO). Peak oil is a scientific analysis and modeling of data. While some in the press report of the peak *theory*, Chris Nelder recently said. "More data might correct existing models, but there is no theory to prove or disprove... peak oil is not about "running out of crude," it's about the *rate* of oil production." [15]

American production has in fact been on the downswing since 1970, just before OPEC emerged as the dominant player. The legendary T. Boone Pickens, an oil tycoon, is one of several Texans who are pushing the peak oil issue of oil scarcity into the mainstream. He believes humans will soon use up half the oil they can extract. Oil production rates will drop, never to recover. Some scientists believe that world production has already peaked, others say we are close (between 2009-2012), and a few dispute it. The real point is not exactly when or if the peak has occurred, but recognizing that it will occur and how we shall prepare for it. This is what the majority of people have not understood or don't want to believe – that the precious oil we depend on will be running out sooner or later.

The following chart shows U.S. production since 1973 to present, compliments of WTRG Economics:

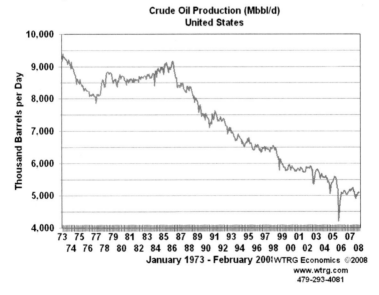

WTRG Economics explains that in 1981 there were 43,887 oil wells drilled compared to 14,447 in 2007. If oil prices remain above $100 per barrel, the number of oil wells completed in 2008 will easily top 17,000, and may approach 18,000. The number of rigs targeting oil is the highest in a decade and the number of successful oil wells is greater than at anytime since 1988. However, even as we drill more, we have been finding less and producing less. Will the crude production continue to fall, even with new drilling, as illustrated in the chart above? Most experts think so – even if there is a short reprieve and some short-term increases, the downswing and depletion is clear. Remember, the U.S. holds only 2% of the worldwide reserves and we consume 25% of oil produced worldwide. Oil worldwide is depleting and will, if it has not yet already, reached its peak and will decline as well.

A perfect example of the debate over declining supply and peak oil is illustrated with two former top executives at Saudi ARAMCO (now both consultants): the former second-in-command, Mr. al-Husseini, says the world faces a brute reality of depleting resources and ever-rising prices, while the former oil reservoir manager, Mr. Saleri, says that with ingenuity and investment, plenty more petroleum can be found and produced. Al-Husseini believes that most of the big oil repositories have been found and no amount of technology will help. (A number of experts tend to concur). "The fact is, we have to work harder and harder to get the oil we need", he said. He counsels that oil conservation will be the primary source of overall availability, while Mr. Saleri believes technology will revive declining oil fields and help find new ones. [16]

Of the 11 OPEC countries, only one increased production since September 2005, and that was a bump of 30,000 barrels per day from Libya. All others declined a total of 2 million barrels per day. Saudi's peak production was in 1979, when they produced nearly 10 million barrels a day. Is the decline voluntary and part of conservation, or is it involuntary? We don't know, but there is speculation.

The largest oil reservoirs are mature, and their production is falling. Approximately **three-quarters of the world's current oil production are from fields that are two or more decades old, past their peaks and beginning declines**. Much of the remaining quarter of production comes from fields that are 10 to 15 years old. New fields are diminishing in number and size every year, and this trend has held for over a decade. [17]

In fact, half of all oil produced comes from just .03% of all fields – as *Profit from the Peak* authors point out, "this is significant because the largest fields are few in number, and when they are past their peaks, then so is the world." [18] In a study on the world's giant oil fields, authority Matthew Simmons found (in 2002) that the average age of the 14 largest fields was 43.5 year old (typically a large field declines after 50); the average age of the 19 largest fields was 70 years old! [19] Twenty years ago, 15 fields had the capacity to produce more than one million barrels per day. Today only four fields can produce that much (Ghawar in Saudi Arabia, Kirkuk in Iraq, Burgan in Kuwait, and Cantarell in Mexico). "In April 2006, a Saudi ARAMCO spokesman admitted that its mature fields are now declining at a rate of 8% per year, implying that Ghawar may have peaked." [20] On a trip to Saudi Arabia, author Paul Roberts caught wind of the same, when he learned that they are using water injection to help force oil out, typically a measure used when oil has depleted past a certain stage.[21] Even in Britain's North Sea, oil production is dwindling, having peaked in 1999 at 2.6 million barrels per day. Today, production is 1.4 million to 1.6 million barrels per day.[22]

"A growing number of oil-industry chieftains are endorsing an idea long deemed fringe: The world is approaching a practical limit to the number of barrels of crude oil that can be pumped every day… That could set the stage for a period marked by energy shortages, high prices and bare-knuckled competition for fuel…The emergence of a production ceiling would mark a monumental shift in the energy world." [23]

A study by ASPO-Netherlands in June 2007 concluded that total world exports have been on a plateau since 2004 despite production increases; exports from non-OPEC countries have declined since 2004; and OPEC exports increased to the end of 2005, followed by a plateau and then slow decline, mainly due to Saudi Arabia. [24]

In a press release in late June of 2008, the Energy Information Administration (EIA) said crude oil production from non-OPEC countries will not be able to keep up with growing global demand in the next few years, forcing oil consuming nations to rely more on OPEC. In its long-term energy forecast, the EIA lowered its estimate of non-OPEC oil production in 2010 to 51.8 million barrels per day, down 1.1 million bpd from last year's forecast. For the same period, OPEC oil output was cut by just 400,000 bpd to 37.4 million. Overall, world energy consumption is forecast to grow 50% by 2030, with demand from developing countries rising 85% compared with a 19% increase in industrialized countries, the EIA said.

What are the estimated reserves worldwide, and how are they measured? Reserves are predicted in three ways: knowing how much oil has been extracted over a period of time (cumulative); estimating the amount that remains to produce (reserves); and estimating the amount of oil that remains to be discovered in the field. To establish the numbers, many technical and scientific methods are used (drilling tests, sensors, seismic readings, etc.) It is part art and part science, and the methods have become more accurate over the years with better technologies.

However, statements of oil reserves have been political and in some cases suspect. For instance, the Soviet Union had a long history of wildly overstating reserves because it increased its image of strength. "...In 1996, *World Oil* estimated the Former Soviet Union reserves at 190 billion barrels, but *Oil and Gas Journal* gave it only 57 billion." [25] For OPEC producers, the motivation was drilling quotas. The permissible production quota was based on a percentage of the reserves held. In some cases, stated reserves doubled or tripled overnight in the 1980's.

The following chart, sourced from the U.S. Geological Survey, shows their estimated world reserves:

World Oil Reserves millions of barrels	
Saudi Arabia	261,750
Canada	180,000
Iraq	115,000
United Arab Emirates	97,800
Kuwait	96,500
Iran	89,700
Venezuela	77,685
Russia	48,573
Libya	29,500
Mexico	26,941
Source: U.S. Geological Survey	

Canada recently moved up from number 20 to number 2 in global oil reserves because of the tar sands. Fuel from the tar sands account for about 26 per cent of Canada's oil production, but by 2025 that figure could possibly grow to 70 per cent. Oil from tar sands is generally difficult and expensive to extract, and it is thicker and harder to refine. **Tar sands** (also referred to as oil sands) are a combination of clay, sand, water, and **bitumen**, a heavy black viscous oil (sort of like asphalt). Tar sands are mined and processed to extract the oil-rich bitumen, which is then refined into oil. The bitumen in tar sands cannot be pumped from the ground in its natural state; instead tar sand deposits are mined, usually using strip mining or open pit techniques; or the oil could be extracted by underground heating (which takes enormous energy and heat) with additional upgrading (in situ) which is not yet well developed. Tar sands are found in 70 countries world wide, including the United States, with some found in eastern Utah.

Oil is not produced from tar sands on any significant commercial level in the United States; in fact, only Canada has a large-scale commercial tar sands industry, with a small amount of oil from tar sands produced in Venezuela. The Canadian tar sands industry is centered in Alberta, and output is expanding. Approximately 20% of U.S. crude oil and products come from Canada, and a substantial portion of this amount comes from tar sands. Canadian tar sands are different than U.S. tar sands in that Canadian tar sands are water wetted, while U.S tar sands are hydrocarbon wetted; hence extraction techniques are different.

So could oil from tar sands help us in the short term? At maximum levels of production, oil from tar sands would account for a mere 4% of the current global oil consumption or 2.5% of the IEA's forecasts by 2025. That is, as noted in *Profit from the Peak*, about the same amount of oil lost to field depletion. So while it can help in the short-term to alleviate some of the supply crisis – and we need all the help we can get - it is not an answer.

Oil Shale is often discussed in the same breath as tar sands, as the sands are known as bituminous sands and oil shale has bituminous materials in it. Oil shale generally refers to sedimentary rock that contains the solid bituminous kerogen which releases petroleum-like liquids when heated. When heated to several hundred degrees

31

Fahrenheit (referred to as "retorting"), an oil-like substance is obtained from the rock which then can be refined into a transportation fuel. The fact that large quantities of heat (energy) are required to obtain a usable fuel from the rock means that this is a far less efficient source of energy than conventional oil.

The term "oil shale" is actually a misnomer, since the rock is not necessarily shale and its kerogen is not crude oil. Oil shale is generally considered to be a 'source material' or an immature oil, younger than tar sands. In a number of countries, shale is mined and directly burned into a low grade fuel to generate electricity, especially in Estonia. Estonia has a large 2000-plus megawatt plant; Brazil, Germany, Israel and China also use oil shale as fuel sources for generation on a smaller scale. In China and Estonia oil shale is also used to make small amounts of liquid fuel. Estonia accounts for about 70% of the oil shale mining - they have no true fossil resources for electric generation. The United States actually holds the world's largest known concentration of oil shale. More than 70 percent of American oil shale — including the thickest and richest deposits — lies on federal land, primarily in Colorado, Utah, and Wyoming, the largest known as the Green River Formation,

Should this be exciting? Why aren't we getting this oil? Access to the richest oil-shale deposits is tricky and difficult to access, the costs are very high and not all deposits are recoverable. The process is quite complicated and expensive, and has also raised concerns about air and water pollution. Oil companies actually began looking for ways to extract oil from shale decades ago, but many efforts were shelved in the 1980s as oil prices fell and supplies stabilized. Some believe it is not ideal because large amounts of water are needed; because much energy is needed for high heat in the process; and because the actual mining can devastate lands with other implications. Chris Nelder says, "After four decades of fully authorized, commercial, even subsidized attempts to develop oil shale into a usable fuel, no one has ever been able to make it economically feasible…it takes an enormous amount of energy to turn it into something usable." [26]

James D. Hamilton, a professor at the University of California, San Diego who has closely followed the shale story for thirty years, has said, "It's remarkable that for over thirty years, the claim has always been that the projects would become economical if the price of oil went up just a little higher. I've watched oil prices go up, and then it turns out the projects still won't fly." [27] Two examples: Shell recently withdrew one of its three permits on oil shale projects because of cost overruns. An Italian oil group working on a large field in Kazakhstan announced that costs were double from the initial estimate just to get it to the initial phase in 2011.

In fact, the standard joke in the industry is the following saying: *Shale oil – fuel of the future, and always will be.* (Note: shale oil is different from the natural gas deposits found and being extracted from shale fields in Texas and Oklahoma, such as from the Barnett Shale and Woodford Shale).

What about Alaska and the Gulf of Mexico and opening new drilling? If new drilling areas were opened, it would not be a short-term or long-term fix - "Is it going to happen overnight? No," said Dan Naatz, vice president of the Independent Petroleum Association of America. "Is it going to solve all of our nation's energy problems? No." [28]

Chris Nelder says we have to be careful not to labor under the mistaken belief that the U.S. can somehow drill its way out of dependency on foreign oil, or that increased domestic production could the relieve today's high prices. [29]

In fact, a number of experts say that as time goes by, the quality of the remaining oil is less and the difficulty in acquiring it is more. Peter Tertzakian is a chief energy economist at ARC Financial Corporation, a leading energy investment firm and former geophysicist with the Chevron Corporation. He says we are not immediately running out of oil but we are "running short of cheap oil, especially the desirable grade of oil that flows easily and is devoid of sulfer, otherwise known as light sweet crude. Our reliance on that cheap oil runs deeper and is more entrenched than most of us are aware…"[30] What we will have remaining is deeper or more difficult to obtain oil, tar sands and shale, lower quality crudes, crude in smaller fields and sometimes politically unsafe or difficult-to-reach areas.

As we have learned from EIA and other sources, world demand for oil is expected to increase by 54 per cent in the first 25 years of the 21st century. To meet that demand, the world's oil-producing countries will have to pump out an additional 44 million barrels of oil each and every day by 2025. [31] Can it be done? There are doubts. The EIA said that crude oil production from non-OPEC countries will not be able to keep up with growing global demand in the next few years, forcing oil consuming nations to rely more on OPEC. In its long-term energy forecast, the EIA lowered its estimate of non-OPEC oil production in 2010 to 51.8 million barrels per day, down 1.1 million bpd from last year's forecast. For the same period, OPEC oil output was cut by just 400,000 bpd to 37.4 million.

The OPEC President, Chakib Khelil, said to journalists on June 24th, 2008 that oil prices will not come down immediately, and that the oil cartel "has done what it can do" to help alleviate the current rising prices. Further, he said, when addressed about the rising prices, "It's impossible to predict. Anything could happen. All I can say is that prices will be high, and will remain high until the end of the year." [32]

The "Hirsch Report", as it has become know, is a respected study on mitigation strategies for peak oil and was published in February 2005. Robert Hirsch, the project leader, along with two other experts had the task of determining when we need to take action to deal with peak oil and the challenges ahead. In their opening pages, they state that "the peaking of world oil production presents the U.S. and the world with an unprecedented risk management problem. As peaking is approached, liquid fuel prices and price volatility will increase dramatically and without timely mitigation, the economic, social and political costs will be unprecedented. Viable mitigation options exist… but they must be initiated more than a decade in advance of peaking…" [33]

Estimates for replacing some of the oil and gas with renewables and alternate sources range from 10% to 30% substitution by 2020 to 2050. A 2006 study sponsored by the Council on Foreign Relations called "National Security Consequences of U.S. Oil Dependency" reached this conclusion: "During the next twenty years (and quite probably beyond) it is infeasible to eliminate the nation's dependence on foreign energy sources."[34]

Energy analyst Paul Horsnell, former Oxford economics lecturer who spent 11 years with the Oxford Institute for Energy Studies and is now with Barclays, said in December 2007 that he "is confident that 2008 will be the seventh straight year of price increases..." He doesn't expect the fundamentals that are driving up prices to change anytime soon. "No massive new sources of energy are likely to come on stream. Other options such as Canadian tar sands are environmentally ruinous, or in the case of biofuels produced from corn, push up food prices." He sees no relief, and doubts that major increases in supply will come forth, either. [35]

Several energy experts have put forth the "Break Point" scenario - that is, the struggle over oil prices, its implications on the economies and societies, and major changes that will occur to meet the challenges once we reach the so-called break point. This would include significant market responses toward alternative fuels and technologies.[36] "The current high oil price may be a demand shock triggered by what had been several years of excellent global economic growth, and thus more benign than supply shocks caused by 1970s-style disruptions," writes CERA's Yergin in the May 28 issue of the Financial Times. Oil prices at this level take us into a new world—"Break Point"—where the question is not only "How high can the price go?", but also "What will be the response?"[37]

Matthew Simmons, an energy investment banker in Houston and an expert on oil policy, said in the Chicago Tribune, "I truly think we're at one of those turning points where the future's looking so ugly nobody wants to face it," said Matthew Simmons,. "We're not talking some temporary Arab embargo anymore. We're not talking your father's energy crisis." [38]

Essentially, it seems that while in the short term, day-to-day prices will move around, they will most likely stay relatively high. Several experts say they believe prices will stay above $100 a barrel in 2008 and beyond. **These are all facts that an investor must chew on - cash flows in an investment from the sale of oil and gas; will they**

stay high or high enough for the investment to make sense, and for long enough?

Also, after reading all of this information, you might be thinking that oil is running out so why invest? It is for several reasons: good drilling programs can have a payout (return of the equity invested) by about 5 years, some much earlier. Oil and gas is not disappearing in 5 or 10 years, or longer. But due to all of the information presented in this chapter, you can see how the prices will probably stay high enough with the commodity in demand for the investment to make sense. Twenty, thirty or forty years from now, the point may be moot and the opportunity gone.

One last important point to understand in our chapter about the state of oil and gas is that there is an **immense transfer of wealth** occurring to the oil producing countries. This transfer shall continue to occur as long as there is oil and gas dependence, and it is running at about **$7 billion dollars a day,** according to Stephen Jen, chief currency economist at Morgan Stanley.[39] The longer-term wealth transfer, if the world follows its current path, is especially destined to those countries with the largest reserves. Those oil-rich nations are taking equity positions in such companies as Citigroup and buying landmarks like the Chrysler Building, to name but two of many recent transactions.

I recognize that this same transfer of wealth came to the U.S. early when it was the number one producer and exporter, and recognize that the wealth generated and its applications expanded our economy and our power greatly. However, the point here is that as other countries gain tremendous wealth from petroleum it tips political power and makes us less effective as a world player. For instance, Iran's government and the nuclear situation – they can be less vulnerable to sanctions designed to pressure it into giving up its nuclear program and in general can be emboldened from their oil wealth. Another example is Russia. As reported by the Washington Post, when Vladimir Putin came to power in 2000, less than two years after the collapse of the ruble and Russia's default on its international debt, the country's policymakers worried that 2003 could bring another financial crisis. However, due to oil revenues, they have paid off their foreign debt, have the third-largest gold and hard-currency reserves in the world (about $425 billion) and have built up a $150 billion rainy-day account called the Stabilization Fund. "The government is much stronger, much more self-assured and self-confident," said Vladimir Milov, head of the Institute of Energy Policy in Moscow and a former deputy minister of energy. "It believes it can cope with any economic crisis at home." This power has contributed to more assertive actions such as trying to reclaim former Soviet republics as part of its sphere of influence and resisting what it views as American expansionism, particularly regarding NATO enlargement and U.S. missile defense in Eastern Europe, and it can even forge an independent approach to contentious issues like Iran's nuclear program.[40]

If we realize that we as a country do not make changes and decrease foreign dependence through a multitude of actions and alternative energies, one of the outcomes is that we give away more and more power as a world player and give away more wealth that could be kept within our borders to work on our somewhat weakened state. "In the United States, the rising bill for imported petroleum lowers already anemic consumer savings rates, adds to inflation, worsens the trade deficit, undermines the dollar and makes it more difficult for the Federal Reserve to balance its competing goals of fighting inflation and sustaining growth."[41]

Let's examine a summary of **other sources of energy at work today** in the U.S. to help us put oil and gas in perspective.

According to the Energy Information Administration, Americans used renewable energy sources—water (hydroelectric), geothermal, wind, sun (solar), and biomass—**which met about 7% of our total energy needs in 2006.** The EIA, by the way, was created in 1977 as the statistical arm of the Department of Energy, charged with developing and analyzing energy data to enhance the understanding of the energy industry.

Of the total renewable energy used in 2005 and 2006, electricity producers consumed 63% while the remaining 37% of renewable energy was biomass consumed for industrial applications (principally paper-making) by plants producing only heat and steam. Biomass is also used for some transportation fuels (ethanol) and to provide some residential and commercial space heating. Renewable-generated electricity comes from hydroelectric energy (75%), followed by biomass (14%), wind (7%), geothermal (4%), and solar (0.1%). Wind-generated electricity increased by almost 21% in 2007 from 2006, more than any other energy source. Some believe that wind has huge potential and may be the most cost effective. Its growth rate was followed closely by solar, which increased by 19% in 2007 over 2006.

The American Wind Energy Association speculates that this barely tapped resource could provide 20 percent of U.S. power by 2020. T. Boone Pickens in the summer of 2008 made the first down payment on 500 wind turbines ($2m each). The order is the first step towards his goal of building the world's largest wind farm, and over the next four years he intends to erect 2,700 turbines across 200,000 acres of the Texan panhandle. This is five times bigger than the world's current record-holding wind farm and when finished will supply 4,000 megawatts of electricity - enough to power about one million homes. "The fact that Pickens, a tycoon who made his fortune in oil, has turned his attention to wind power is an indication of how the tectonic plates are moving. Until recently wind was seen as marginal and alternative; now it is being eyed by Wall Street," says The Guardian.[42]

Many U.S. states or private companies haven't waited for the federal government to jump-start programs. Florida Power and Light (FPL) announced plans recently to build three solar energy plants in Florida, including one that would be the largest of its kind. Costing $688 million, they will represent the first commercial-scale renewable energy sites in the Sunshine State. [43] FPL is also a top wind generator. Texas officials approved a $4.9 billion plan to add transmission lines for wind powered energy. Google announced it will build a 1.6 megawatt solar installation on their campus, and California signed legislation making solar panels a standard option for new home buyers by 2011. By the way, the Sharp plant in Kameyama, Japan is the largest solar installation to date with 5.2 megawatt capacity. Japan accounts for

48 percent of the globe's solar-power generation -- compared with 15 percent in the United States.[44]

When it comes to powering our cars and transport vehicles – and transportation accounts for **more than half of global oil demand and continues to account for more than 95 percent of all the energy used for transportation in the United States**, says the EIA - there are various energy sources but no major replacement to gasoline yet. Rising oil prices are definitely bringing increased attention to alternative fuels and technologies. "**Alternative-fuel" vehicles do not burn gasoline**. Instead, they are powered by electricity, propane, natural gas, methanol or ethanol. **"Flex-fuel" vehicles run on gasoline and other fuels**. **"Hybrids" combine two propulsion systems** -- electricity with a small diesel or gasoline engine that acts as a generator when the battery runs low.

Here is a summary as it stands today, at this writing:

* **Biodiesel** has been a grass roots oil replacement but there are issues of use in lower temperatures, because it easily thickens and needs additives (below 40 degrees). Biodiesel, made from vegetable oils or animal fats and even algae, is biodegradable and releases 75% less carbon emissions (though some say it smells very bad). One advantage is that is can be used in standard diesel engines. However, simply being "renewable" does not automatically make a fuel better for the atmosphere than the fossil fuel it replaces. The European Union was recently shocked to learn that some of its imported biodiesel, derived from palm trees planted on rain-forest lands, was more than twice as bad for climate warming as petroleum diesel. Most biodiesel companies at this time are outside of the U.S.

* **Propane** is the most used gas alternative in the U.S. with more than 200,000 vehicles, mostly fleet vehicles. However, it is not considered a good alternative because it is produced as a byproduct of natural gas and petroleum refining, and subject to many of the issues at hand over oil and gas. Most people call liquefied petroleum gas (LPG) "propane", because LPG is mostly made up of propane. Actually, LPG is made of a mixture of propane and other similar types of hydrocarbon

gases. Besides being a byproduct of natural gas and oil refining with the inherent problems, other downsides are the propane tank required, that the exhaust smells bad, and that propane prices are almost the same as gas.

* **Natural Gas.** It is mostly comprised of methane (one carbon atom and four hydrogen atoms), is drawn up from underground wells just like oil, and is processed to remove byproducts. Natural gas is one of the cheaper and cleaner-burning fossil fuels. How does a natural gas vehicle work? The gas is stored in cylinders installed in the rear, under carriage, or on the roof of the vehicle. Inside the cylinders, the gas is under high pressure -- between 3,000 and 3,600 pounds per square inch. When gas is required, it travels through a fuel regulator located in the engine compartment and is then injected through a specially designed mixer, to get the correct air-to-gas mixture.

Retrofits are necessary for natural gas to work in gasoline cars, with very high pressure needed. To accommodate these high pressure requirements, the vehicles are equipped with specially constructed high pressure storage tanks to contain the fuel, along with pressure regulators that step-down the final delivery pressure for the fuel metering system There are strong safety concerns (and fears). The technology required, as well as the need for a natural gas refueling infrastructure are current barriers to the widespread use of natural gas vehicles in the United States. The driving range is less than one half of a gasoline-powered vehicle. And of course, the issues over oil and gas laid out in this book directly affect natural gas.

* **Ethanol** is the most well-known gas alternative. Favored by some Midwestern farmers, ethanol is usually blended with gasoline. Corn-based in the U.S., ethanol is usually used in "flex-fuel" vehicles— vehicles that can be run on either gasoline or ethanol. An estimated 2.5 million ethanol flex-fuel vehicles exist in the US today, but only a small percentage actually are using ethanol, as it is not widely available yet. There were some press reports in 2008 that ethanol blended without the additive does not burn well and vaporous residue with carbon deposits clogs up inside the valves. More frequent oil changes are necessary or there can be big problems with the engine and ventilation systems.[45]

The hopeful promise of ethanol is not really panning out on another score and this is more important. It turns out that it takes more energy to produce ethanol that what is gotten from it. It takes 22,000 BTUs to create a gallon of gas, which has 12,000 BTUs, whereas it takes 98,000 BTU's to make a gallon of ethanol, which contains 76,000 BTUs. (A BTU or British Thermal Unit is defined as the amount of energy required to raise the temperature of one pound of water one degree Fahrenheit, starting from 60 degree Fahrenheit.) Some further points made in a scholarly group study revealed that ethanol produces only 12% less greenhouse gases than gasoline; 99% of corn is fertilized and the required nitrogen fertilizers, herbicides and pesticides are all made from fossil fuels; and corn erodes soil 18 times faster than it can reform.[46] Those are but a few facts laid out in a paper by a number of experts on the subject. Professor Tad Patzek, a chemical engineer at UC Berkeley, calls the ethanol effort a politically driven initiative by confused people who think it is good for the country. "We need a new liquid fuel, but this isn't the one," says Professor David Pimentel of Cornell University, who collaborated with Patzek on the study.[47] And according to a 2007 study at Arizona State University, a gallon of corn-based ethanol requires 785 gallons of water to irrigate and grow, while a gallon of gas used 2.5 gallons of water in its refining process. This is no small matter either.

Let's add one more issue to the mix about ethanol before moving on. The increase in corn prices created through demand for making ethanol has spilled over to the food supply: this affects everyone, including poorer countries who need corn, regular consumers who pay more at the grocery store, and farmers (dairy, poultry and livestock industries) who use corn-based animal feed. Subsequently a rise in the price of meats and poultry follows to compensate. "When we talk about the influence of biofuels on the economy of grains, we are talking about the corn from the U.S., not the sugar cane from Brazil," said Abdolreza Abbassian, secretary of the Intergovernmental Group on Grains within Food and Agriculture Organization of the United Nations (FAO).[48] A recent study by the International Monetary Fund shows that Brazil's ethacane hasn't been responsible for higher international food prices.[49]

The Federal Reserve Bank reported in their 2008 Monetary Policy Report that last year's increase in the PCE price index for food and beverages, at 4 1/2 percent, was the largest in nearly two decades. Food prices accelerated in response to strong world demand and high demand for corn for the production of ethanol. Ethanol production is now taking roughly one-third of the U.S. corn crop, according to the American Petroleum Institute. This percentage is expected to increase over the next several years. There may be some promise in cellulosic ethanol made from wood chips, wheat straw, etc., though this type of ethanol does not break down easily. Ethanol doesn't seem to be a solution.

* **Hydrogen** has been talked up but has yet to make an impact – though there were several announcements in summer of 2008, at press time of this book, which are showing development. Hydrogen can be made by nuclear and alternative power sources and auto makers are testing the technology. However, unlike propane which is a waste product of the gasoline manufacturing process, hydrogen is an end product requiring lots of high-cost energy to make (not to mention the major increase in carbon dioxide air-pollution produced during its manufacture). Both factors make hydrogen less favored. "In the end, about 80 percent of the original energy generated in order to produce hydrogen is lost..." [50] Weather and air temperatures can be an issue - water is both a byproduct and a necessity for the production of fuel cells, and the risk of freezing conditions in the winter is a very real problem that must be addressed. Safety issues of handling pressurized hydrogen are just as serious as it sounds, too.

The technical challenges in making, storing, and transporting hydrogen, as well as using it in conventional internal combustion engines or in fuel cell vehicles seem rather overwhelming, according to a number of experts. However, BMW has a model out. Honda announced in June 2008 that it has begun the first commercial production ever of a hydrogen fuel cell-powered car, which will be available on a limited basis in California. The four-door sedan, called the FCX Clarity, runs on electricity from a fuel cell battery that is powered by hydrogen fuel. Steam is the car's only byproduct. The car reportedly will get the equivalent of about 74 mpg of a gas-powered car and can be driven for about 280 miles before needing to be refueled. While the U.S. Department of Energy has been a proponent of hydrogen fuel as an alternative energy for cars, there are currently few hydrogen-fuel filling stations the U.S. Forbes reports that what makes Honda's gambit significant is the corresponding release of its *Home Energy Station Unit*, which can be set up in the yard at home. It uses natural gas to produce enough hydrogen to power the Clarity and your home at around 50% of the normal cost and with a 30% reduction in emissions.[51] Toyota has made some major developments with their Advanced **Fuel Cell Hybrid Vehicle** with a newly designed high performance fuel cell stack. Just certified in Japan for road use on June 3, 2008, the new design reportedly results in 515 miles on a single fueling. Toyota engineers apparently focused their attention on the building block of the stack, called Membrane Electrode Assembly (MEA), with a basic yet persistent problem of internally produced water interfering with electrical generation. Fuel efficiency gains were made by improving fuel performance, enhancing the regenerative brake system and reducing energy consumed by the auxiliary system. They worked at incorporating degradation control for the electrode catalyst, improving fuel cell durability and developed better high pressure hydrogen storage tanks.

Some become confused between electric batteries and batteries using hydrogen fuel cells. What is the difference? Using hydrogen fuel cells to power vehicles is much like using a battery to power a car. However, the difference is the source of the power. Batteries must be recharged from another source, namely electricity. Fuel cells depend upon a chemical process, using hydrogen fuel and oxygen, to supply their power. The term *cell* is relevant to the process as well. Because a single cell would not emit enough power to run a vehicle, a number of cells must be used together to form a *cell stack*. To be clear, fuel cells are different from batteries in that they consume reactant, (which must be replenished) whereas batteries store electrical energy chemically in a closed system. Additionally, while the electrodes within a battery react and change as a battery is charged or discharged, a fuel cell's electrodes are catalytic and relatively stable.

* Battery power is being used to complement gasoline engines and boost fuel economy in hybrids. Battery power will continue to be developed in conjunction with gas or other fuels (PHEV stands for Plug-in Hybrid Electric Vehicles), and may be one of the most promising solutions to personal transportation. Public demand for the hybrid Toyota Prius, which reportedly can get 50 miles per gallon, has outpaced production since it was introduced in 2001 with frequent waiting lists, and it is apparently the number 2 car in the world right now. The Hybrid engine has two parts: the electric engine powered by batteries and usually a 4 or 6 cylinder gas engine. When turned on, the gas engine doesn't start up, which is great for city driving - when you're not moving, the engine isn't idling. When the batteries run low, the gas engine turns itself on. The electric engine is fine at low speeds but not at highway speeds. At about 40 MPH, at least currently with the Prius, the gas engine turns on. Current and new hydrids can be found with a number of car makers such as Saturn, Chevy, Ford and even Lexus. Other car makers, including Mercedes, have announced that they are working on hybrids and electric cars for the near future.

The future of **solely powered battery-electric vehicles** (BEVs as opposed to PHEVs) should be, by all counts, excellent. Automakers shifted focus away from BEVs a decade ago, which seems short-sighted and not comprehensible. (I'll bet GM is kicking themselves as they see what Toyota has done with the Prius, and as they slip into, as is reported in the press "potential bankruptcy" - they had some well-received EV-1 battery cars just a handful of years ago but pulled them. They are now working to introduce the Chevy Volt for 2011). Critics say that an issue with EVs is that they (currently) only have about 100 miles per charge (+/-), though for urban areas or for those who commute less that that per day, this is probably not an issue. Batteries can save wasted energy and they generate no tailpipe emissions. If generation of electricity moves to more clean sources (wind, solar, hydrogen, etc.), then the whole concept becomes even better. Driving an electric car will result in about a 95 percent net reduction in pollution compared to a conventional car. The 'get up and go' was already acceptable to many in cars earlier this decade, and is now even better with stronger batteries in test cars. Because there's no internal combustion engine in an electric car, a lot fewer repairs are needed. No timing belts, water pumps, radiators, fuel injectors, or exhaust systems means fewer visits to a mechanic. No tune-ups or oil change required, either. But consumers will pay more up front, due to the high cost of most electric vehicles.

Some automakers have been quoted as saying that consumers have a hard time understanding or even wanting an electric car. It seems rather short-sighted to say this. Perhaps, or perhaps not. Perhaps unless or until events change their minds, like the sustained high price of gas or less supply of it or perhaps until consumers are educated about them (or any alternate, for that matter). J.D. Power & Associates released study results in July 2008 that 62% of people researched plan to buy a hydrid in the next two years (which increased 50% from last years study. Interest in ethanol dropped substantially, the same report showed).

Highway-safe BEVs are tangible for several reasons. Battery technologies have reached the tipping point (and will continue to improve) in terms of sufficient range and costs. And because of the success of hybrids, many U.S. consumers are becoming comfortable with the ride and reliability of battery-powered vehicles." [52] A breakthrough invention for battery systems on all-electric cars actually recharges the battery through braking and accelerating (regenerative acceleration). [53]

A handful of start-up companies as well as traditional car makers are building products that may be available as early as 2009, it seems. The sexy Tesla Roadster is among the test cars. Battery-power is an area that many are excited about since the potential benefits are high, and word is that lithium-battery makers will be able to succeed.

The authors of *Profit from the Peak* say, "It's easy to see how an all-electric economy could be the only possible, practical response to the peaking of our traditional forms of energy. Not only does it open the door to emerging and enormous renewable resources like geothermal, solar, wind and marine energy, but it has the potential to eliminate most of the carbon emissions of the fossil-fueled regime...Most analysts who are aware of the energy issues that underpin "peak everything" have arrived at this same conclusion, even petroleum geologists." [54]

The Brookings Institute held a conference in Washington D.C., June 2008 regarding electric vehicles. There was much information relayed but something of note here: it was reported that Israel announced their government initiative to go to electric cars within 10 years, and the CEO of carmakers Renault and Nissan committed to make fast, fun and full-sized fully electric cars for mass production by 2011. As reported by Shai Agassi, the government is committed to the infrastructure of plug-in generators at parking lots and where needed, but a second part of the approach for longer distances needed is a replaceable battery. The driver would stop at a facility (much like a car wash or filling station) to drop out the battery and replace it with a new one. There is government support, tax incentives, and private equity investors for the initiative. Shortly afterwards, Denmark committed to the same thing.[55]

Sweden is testing solar-run podcars and **solar technology for personal transport** is also being addressed with some very interesting possibilities to come. Those are the alternatives for **personal transportation** as it stands today. I am a believer in American ingenuity and hope that it will shine through and win the day over political situations to help find solutions to our overall energy crisis, but I realize – and I hope everyone who reads this will realize - that we cannot get out of long-term crisis situation by simply drilling more or figuring that politicians will wake up one day early enough to plan for and to make an impact on the impending crisis. It might seem odd for a book about oil and gas investments to state this. I take the chiding that James Kunstler wrote in his book, "How could such a catastrophe be so close at hand and civilized, educated people in free countries with free news media and transparent institutions be so uninformed about it…Mostly it is a matter of cultural inertia, aggravated by collective delusion, nursed in…complacency…We believe that the world is full of enormous amounts of as-yet-undiscovered oil fields…the thinking stops there…A parallel idea seemed to prevail across the nation – and across the political spectrum – that there was no need to worry about oil and gas because some other fuel or system or technology will come along… to save our asses." [56]

As you read through the issues in this chapter and beyond, we will see that no matter how much we love oil and gas, no matter how much we depend on it and likewise see it as a good investment, we are entering into the beginning of the slow and drawn-out end. Oil prices will most likely remain high though fluctuate in this era, as the precious fuel becomes more scarce, and that is why it seems an opportune time to invest.

The U.S. oil and gas industry invested an estimated $98 billion between 2000 and 2005 into emerging energy technologies including renewables, frontier hydrocarbons, such as shale and oil sands, and end-use technologies, such as fuel cells. This investment represents almost 75 percent of the total $135 billion spent by all of industry and the federal government combined on emerging energy technologies during this time period, according to a May 2006 study by the Institute for Energy Research (IER) and the Center for Energy, says the American Petroleum Institute. Consumers need more choices while slowly decreasing the full-on requirement for oil. It has been stated that the CEO of a major oil company believes that even after accounting for technological breakthroughs, renewables could only make up about 30 percent of the total energy supply by midcentury.

I agree with the authors of "*The Oil Factor*" when they wrote that looking back over the last 40 years, reading the speeches and white papers and opinion pieces, "it is hard not to feel incredibly frustrated that no one paid more attention. If the political will had existed during the last three decades to do more than pay lip service to alternative energies – if by today, for instance, as Carter had proposed, wind energy accounted for significant portion of our energy usage or if we had launched large-scale programs to develop more efficient solar cells – well, it's hard to overstate how much better off we'd be, and the world as well. We didn't, however, and nothing can turn back the clock." [57]

"If the U.S. government and its citizens decided to launch a new energy system and have it in place within twenty years [*or ten years, I might add*], not only would the energy system be built, but the rest of the world would be forced to follow along," says Paul Roberts. "Instead, American policymakers are too paralyzed to act, terrified that to change U.S. energy patterns would threaten the nation's economy and geopolitical status – not to mention outrage voters…The energy superpower has not only surrendered its once-awesome edge…but made it less and less likely that an effective solution…will be deployed in time."[58] In fact, other countries are taking steps ahead of us in solutions.

Here is an odd thing for a book on oil and gas to say, but since this is a book about investments, I say investors should also consider alternative energy programs, not only to hedge their portfolios and to support the need for development, but for the pure opportunity. One foot in the past and present with oil, one foot in the present and future with alternatives. But that is for another book and another time.

Peter Tertzakian discusses the "Energy Cycle", much like the cycles we have in real estate or in the general economy. In simple terms, he says, as prices rise, producers rush more supply to market. During price hikes, businesses and people tend to slow down their consumption. When prices go back down, businesses and people tend to use energy more wastefully. After the 70's energy crises, we were conditioned to buy smaller, more fuel-efficient cars like the Pinto; when a gallon of gas cost less than a gallon of milk in the later 90's, Hummers and SUVs emerged as popular choices. "In addition, during low-price eras, industries do not have the incentive to focus on efficiency or conservation, and energy companies have no interest to invest in more production. As a result, the supply becomes pinched, prices eventually go back up, and the wheel turns again." [59] There is often or sometimes a rebalance to the cycle, but what about when the source is running out, or the sources are becoming more difficult to obtain? There will be consequences. Only 150 years ago, Mr. Tertzakian reminds us, whale oil was the world's primary illuminating fuel, and I will add, horses were a main mode of transportation.

I think the following quote couldn't be any truer: "Trying to maintain business as usual by increasing energy supply may be possible in the short term. But in the long term, it is not only impossible; it's suicidal...but human history has precious few examples of heeding such foresight and proactively preparing for the future. Instead, we invariably cling to the present with a white-knuckled grip and try to ward off undesirable changes as long as possible..." [60] Quoting Peter Tertzakian again, "Our growing addiction to oil is not easily sustainable, if in fact it is sustainable at all, and this means that big changes in the world of energy are coming at you faster than you think." [61] While we often focus our fuel addiction on transportation, food is vitally tied up in all of this. As CNN reported, in the U.S. up to 20 percent of the country's fossil fuel consumption goes into the food chain which points out that fossil fuel use by the food system in the developed world "often rivals that of automobiles". To feed an average family of four in the developed world uses up the equivalent of 930 gallons of gasoline a year - just shy of the 1,070 gallons that same family would use up each year to power their cars.[62]

We moved most recently from a coal-based society in last century; it will be *interesting* (for want of a better word) to see what and how the transition develops in this century. Let's be realistic though: **oil and gas currently fulfils the lions share of our energy needs today and into the foreseeable future.** We are not able to abandon fossil fuels now or for some time (even if we wanted to). Our infrastructure is built around it. It is the primary source of our energy. As John Orban III has said, "With the exception of food and water, oil is the most important commodity in the world. You really can't leave home without it!"[63]

Let us sum up this chapter, concerning the state of oil & gas: we have a situation whereby much of the world and certainly the U.S. is addicted to oil & gas and depends on it; demand grows yet the supply is finite and there are questions about sustaining production; much of the reserves and supply are not found in the U.S., making the situation more vulnerable; alternative sources are slow to come (but needed); there is no meaningful focus or national policy from the government yet; the general population feels the pain but are still addicted to their cars and high use of energy (the highest in the world per capita), and I might add, in general are not well informed about all of this; mix in environmental, economic and political issues abroad with the possible intermittent weather disruptions (as in hurricanes), and what you end up with is a valuable commodity which is volatile and charged with emotion – and isn't going anywhere in the short term.

*"By God, we will have to bloody well change" our over-reliance on oil.
Charles Maxwell, top energy analyst. Businessweek, July 7, 2008
"The Oracle of Oil Speaks" by Roben Farzad*

*"You can't solve a problem with the same kind of thinking that created it."
Albert Einstein*

*"I'd put my money on the sun and solar energy. What a source of power! I hope
we don't have to wait 'til oil and coal run out before we tackle that."
Thomas Edison (1847-1931) compliments of Ronald Swenson*

"My father rode a camel. I drive a car. My son flies a jet. His son will ride a camel."
popular saying in Saudi Arabia

CHAPTER 3:
HISTORY OF OIL & GAS

Thanks to BERA (Business and Economics Research Advisor) for much of the historical background.

The story of oil and gas spans thousands of year and has a long and fascinating history. The development of oil and gas has evolved over time and its uses have also expanded, becoming an integral part of today's global economy. The use of oil eventually replaced coal as the world's primary source of industrial power in the early twentieth century and still remains the critical fuel source that powers industry and transportation.

Many are surprised to hear that ancient cultures used crude oil as a substance for binding materials and as a sealant for waterproofing various surfaces. Five thousand years ago, the Sumerians used asphalt to inlay mosaics in walls and floors. Mesopotamians used bitumen to line water canals, seal joints in wooden boats and to build roads. It was used to preserve mummies. The Bible refers to pitch being used for building purposes -- cementing walls -- in Babylon. Ancient Persian tablets indicate the medicinal and lighting uses of petroleum in the upper levels of their society. By 1500 B.C., techniques for lighting consisted of a fire pan filled with oil made of a certain volatility so that it would burn slowly and not cause uncontrollable flames or explosions.

Over time, the wick oil lamp replaced the fire pan using flammable oil similar to today's kerosene lanterns.

The Chinese were the first to discover underground oil deposits in salt wells, and they quickly recognized the importance and potential use of oil and gas. Around 500 B.C., ancient Chinese history describes wells over 100 feet deep containing water and natural gas along the Tibetan border. The Chinese constructed extensive bamboo pipelines drawing from the wells in order to transport oil and natural gas, used for lighting. By 1500 A.D., the Chinese were exploring and digging wells more than 2,000 feet deep.

Incendiary weapons at sea were used by the Byzantines in the suppression of a revolt against the Emperor Anastasius I in 513 A.D. Around 670 A.D., the Emperor Constantine IV used burning petroleum thrust out from a device onto enemy ships. Romans used flaming containers of oil as weapons. Incendiary or flaming weapons had been used in warfare for centuries prior to the invention of "Greek fire", including a number of petroleum and bitumen-based mixtures; however, Greek fire was difficult to extinguish and could burn on water, making it a devastating invention. "Greek fire" may have been a form of naphtha or another low-density liquid hydrocarbon, as petroleum was known to Eastern chemists long before its use became widespread in the 1800s.

The Romans used oil surface deposits for burning lamps. Petroleum was known as *burning water* in Japan in the 7th century. The Middle East's petroleum industry was established by the 8th century, when the streets of the newly constructed Baghdad were paved with tar, derived from petroleum that became accessible from natural fields in the region. Petroleum was distilled by Persian chemist al-Razi in the 9th century, producing chemicals such as kerosene.

During the mid 13th century in what is now Azerbaijan, in the Persian city of Baku, inhabitants devised methods and collected from oil seeps in the surface. By the mid 1590's, shallow pits of about 115 feet were dug at Baku to facilitate the collecting of oil, which were in essence primitive oil wells. In 1650, Romania was the site of Europe's first commercial oil reservoir. This site was a major source of oil for Europe. More than 200 years later, Ploesti, Romania became the site of the world's first oil refinery. The earliest mention of American petroleum occurs in Sir Walter Raleigh's account of the Trinidad Pitch Lake in 1595; thirty-seven years later, the account a Franciscan, Joseph de la Roche d'Allion, to the oil springs of New York was published in Sagard's *Histoire du Canada*. Oil sands were mined from 1745 in the Alsace region of France by special appointment of Louis XV.

In the early 1800's, merchants built damns that allowed oil to float to the waters' surface in an area within Western Pennsylvania called Oil Creek. A technique was employed by placing blankets in the water, letting them soak with oil, and the oil was then retrieved by wringing out the blankets. In 1849, Abraham Gesner, a Canadian geologist, distilled bituminous tar to produce coal oil, calling it kerosene and eight years later, with the invention of the kerosene burner, it became a highly-desired illuminant (replacing whale oil). Interestingly, in 1854 Benjamin Silliman, a professor at Yale University, was the first to fractionate petroleum by distillation. This discovery rapidly spread around the world, and the first Russian refinery in the mature oil fields at Baku was built in 1861. At that time Baku produced about 90% of the world's oil.

The first American gas well was drilled near Fredonia, NY in 1821, and the first oil well was drilled in 1859 in Pennsylvania by Edwin Drake. The modern oil and gas industry was born in the late 19th century. As Colin Campbell tells us, the Industrial Revolution was already in progress being driven by the steam engine, fuelled by coal. But then in the 1860s, a German engineer found a way to insert the fuel directly into the cylinder inventing the Internal Combustion Engine, which was more efficient. At first, it used benzene distilled from coal, before turning to petroleum refined from crude oil. The first automobile took to the road in 1882 and the first tractor was used in 1907. The cheap and abundant supply of energy changed the world in then unimaginable ways, leading to the rapid expansion of industry, transport, trade and agriculture, which has allowed the population to expand six-fold in parallel. [1]. Today there are more than 600,000 producing oil wells in the US and more than 200,000 gas wells, even though we are not the largest producer. [2]

The invention of the kerosene lamp in the mid 1850's led to the establishment of the first U.S. oil company, the Pennsylvania Rock Oil Company. However, the first major oil company was the Standard Oil Company founded by John D. Rockefeller in 1870. Standard Oil built its first oil refinery in Pennsylvania, then later expanded its extensive operations nationwide. After a decade of fierce competition, Standard Oil became the industry's most dominant company controlling 80 percent of the distribution of all principal oil products, in particular kerosene.

In 1909 as a result of antitrust laws, federal courts ordered the break up of the Standard Oil Company, dividing it up into 34 separate companies. Standard Oil dominated the first two decades of the oil and gas industry, and the U.S. accounted for more than half of the world's production until around 1950. As the industry became more global in nature, other world markets in Europe, Russia and Asia, began to play a much greater role. New industry giants emerged such as Shell, Royal Dutch, and Anglo-Persian which later became British Petroleum. The major companies were founded as follows: Standard Oil Company – founded in 1870; Gulf Oil, in 1890; Texaco, in 1901; Royal Dutch Shell, in 1907; Anglo-Persian Oil Company, in 1909; Turkish Petroleum Company, in 1910.

As the oil industry unfolded over several decades, Standard Oil of New Jersey later became Esso, then Exxon; Standard Oil of New York became Mobil, and Standard Oil of California is now Chevron. Along with Royal Dutch Shell, Texaco, Gulf, and British Petroleum (BP), these oil giants became known as the "seven sisters."

Among the nations that were becoming industrialized, America had the best supplies and was the first to find and market oil in commercial quantities as well a make widespread applications to the infrastructure and transportation. Since then, we have never ceased being the world largest consumer of oil & gas.

World War I marked the beginning of an era where oil played a truly major role. At the beginning of that war, as Peter Tertzakian points out, the British went to France with 827 motorcars and 15 motocycles. By the end of the war, the British had 56,000 trucks, 23,000 automobiles and 34,000 motocycles; they went from 250 planes to 55,000 during the course of the war. It isn't surprising that oil was essential to them. The entry of the U.S. into the war helped tip the balance for the Allies, in part due to oil supplies and reserves that the US brought. Lord Curzon famously said, "The Allies floated to victory on a wave of oil." [3]

The mind-set of post World War II U.S. was that oil would always be there in abundant and unlimited supply. Further, the mind-set was that the America dominated it so forcefully through the U.S. oil companies (with their power and influence), that there were little concerns over security. At that time, about half of the world's reserves were controlled by the U.S. (Today only 6% of worldwide reserves are held by investor-owned oil, non-government controlled companies). In the 1950's, American-based oil companies produced 45% of foreign oil but this has dropped to 10%.

At the beginning of the 20th century, oil production was dominated by three regions: the U.S., Russia and the Dutch East Indies. However, during the first decade of the 20th century, major efforts were underway to explore and develop oil production in the Middle East. Oil exploration began in Persia (what is now Iran) followed by Turkey. In the late 1930's, the Burgan oilfield was discovered in Kuwait. A decade later, the Ghawar oilfield was discovered in Saudi Arabia, and it still remains the largest oil field ever discovered. After World War II, joint American and Saudi commercial oil enterprises were formed creating conglomerates, such as Casco (California Arabian Standard Oil Company) and Caltex (California Texas Oil Company). Eventually, Esso (Exxon) and Mobil joined the Standard Oil Company of California to form Aramco (Arabian American Oil Company).

We have now experienced some 'world oil shocks' due to political and economic situations. The first oil shock occurred in 1973 as a result of the Yom Kippur war in the Middle East. This war and its political effects caused an enormous increase in world oil prices, and showed us a new vulnerability. Oil embargos were instituted during this time period by the oil exporting countries in the region, reducing world oil production. In fact they blocked just 5% of our imported oil, but it resulted in quadrupled prices.[4] After this first oil shock, which resulted in real oil supply shortages for countries targeted by the embargo, the industrialized countries established the International Energy Agency (IEA) in 1974. This agency within the OECD (Organization for Economic Cooperation and Development) was made up of over 20 countries including the U.S., Canada, Western Europe and Japan. (Its objectives are to promote cooperation in reducing dependence on oil, information systems, and ensuring fair and effective management of resources).

The second oil shock occurred in 1979, again causing dramatic increases in world oil prices. This oil shock was the result of the Iranian crisis caused by political and social upheaval in Iran, which led to strikes in most sectors of the economy, in particular the oil industry. Iranian production fell from 6 million barrels per day in September 1978 to 400,000 barrels per day in January 1979. Saudi Arabia initially increased production to compensate for the Iranian supply shortage, but later placed a ceiling on its production. These series of events led to escalating oil prices and uncertainty with the world oil market.

Following these two crises, there was much attention and media coverage about oil supply levels and the concern over oil being a limited resource that would eventually run out. However, a period of increased production and reduced demand caused an oil glut in the 1980s. James Schlesinger, the first U.S. energy secretary, has said for decades that when it comes to energy policy, "the U.S. toggles between complacency and panic."[5] The Energy Cycle as mentioned by Peter Tertzakian illustrates the point well (discussed in the previous chapter).

What is now unfolding is another oil shock, but this one may be more sustained. As the CERA Break Point study points out, "the fact that the world could take $80 per barrel in its stride in the context of strong economic growth does not mean that a price that is 60%

higher at a time of a credit crunch will be so easily assimilated. The economic toll is mounting. Airlines are certainly in shock as they start charging for checked luggage to find a way to pass on their biggest cost. Carmakers are reeling. Retailers are tracking the shrinking wallets of their customers. The rising prices for food reflect, in part, the impact of higher energy costs...Prices at such levels create their own negative effects on the world economy...Consumer confidence plummets and companies suspend decisions on major capital projects. Political leaders plead for energy conservation and driving restrictions are introduced in several major cities." [6] At the end of 2007, as oil was heading towards $100 for the first time, the U.S. Congress passed the first bill requiring an increase in automobile fuel efficiency in 32 years. Consumers now want to buy fuel efficiency instead of SUVs. Hybrids are going from fringe to mainstream and a concerted assault has been launched on the problems of battery technology.

It is important to understand how the energy world has changed, says The American Petroleum Institute (API). Forty years ago, world oil reserves were largely the domain of the investor-owned, international oil companies, based principally in the United States. Most people today assume international or U.S. oil companies are little changed from decades ago, still sitting astride the bulk of these world oil reserves. That is not the case. Today, world oil reserves are 80 percent owned by the national oil companies of foreign governments, many formed during the past 30 years. Only approximately 6 - 10 percent of worldwide oil reserves are now held by investor-owned oil companies. The largest American oil company, Exxon Mobil, is only the 14th largest in the world, and is dwarfed by the really big oil companies--all owned by foreign governments or government-sponsored monopolies--that dominate the world's oil supply.

As API has written on another point, contrary to popular belief, America's oil companies aren't owned just by a small group of insiders anymore. Only 1.5 percent of industry shares are owned by company executives. The rest is owned by tens of millions of Americans, many of them middle class. If you're wondering who owns "Big Oil," chances are the answer is "you do," says API. [7] If you have a mutual fund account or an IRA, there's a good chance it invests in oil and natural gas stocks.

In addition, American-based oil companies produced 45% of foreign oil in the 1950's, but that has dropped to about 10%. Faced with competition, the investor owned oil companies have scaled up within this new world – principally through mergers and acquisitions. Concerning imports, there is an important fact to note. American dependence on foreign imported oil has grown from 10% in 1970 to 65% by 2004. But when you consider supply, it is worse. With 94% of the world's oil supply locked up by foreign governments, some of which is held by countries that may be hostile, the relatively puny American oil companies do not have access to enough crude oil to significantly affect the market. Thus, Exxon Mobil buys 90% of the crude oil that it refines for the U.S. market from the big players. The price at the U.S. pump is rising because the price the big oil companies charge Exxon Mobil and the other American companies for crude oil is going up.[8]

In most major producing countries, the government owns the rights to develop the resources. In the U.S., much of the land is privately-owned and the decision to explore and produce oil is between the land owners and the producing company. **That is a big difference from most of the world, and important for investors to understand – investors in the U.S. have opportunities that many others don't when it comes to direct participation investment programs.**

An interesting comment was made by the 'dean' of oil analysts, Charles Maxwell, on the Charlie Rose show, June 10th, 2008. He said something to the effect that he thinks the large oil companies have now become too large or cumbersome and they are slowly dying, while the young, middle size or smaller oil companies are the future – they are more mobile, flexible and are generally entrepreneurs who can more deftly adjust to the markets.[9] .

To end this chapter on the history of oil and gas, I turn to Paul Roberts who wrote in his book *The End of Oil*, "Historically, shifts from one energy technology to another have proved wrenching. The leaps from wood to coal, and from coal to oil caused economic disruption and political uncertainty (sixteenth century Englishmen nearly revolted at having to burn sooty coal instead of wood). And these were fairly slow-motion transitions…Given that today's infrastructure is even more intertwined with global economics and politics and culture, would a fundamental change in our energy technology be even more disruptive? …And what would a new energy order look like? Will it be better than the one we have, or a hastily arranged stopgap arrangement? Will we be richer or poorer, more powerful or more hampered, happier with our advanced energy technologies, or bitter over our memories of a bygone golden age? And who will be in control? Are the current world powers-most of whom are the biggest consumers of oil – still likely to be the leaders in this brave new world?" [10]

"*The First Law of Petropolitics posits the following: The price of oil and the pace of freedom always move in opposite directions in oil-rich petrolist states... And these negative trends are reinforced by the fact that the higher the price goes, the less petrolist leaders are sensitive to what the world thinks or says about them...The lower the price of crude oil falls, the more petrolist leaders are sensitive to what outside forces think of them.*"

Thomas Friedman, columnist for the New York Times *and author. 2006*

"Drill for oil? You mean drill into the ground to try and find oil? You're crazy!" 1859, drillers whom Edwin Drake tried to enlist for oil drilling

CHAPTER 4:
WHAT IS CRUDE OIL?
HOW IS IT DRILLED? HOW IS IT SOLD?

Oil was formed from the remains of animals and plants that lived millions of years ago. According to geological theory, oil formed over a period of millions of years by decomposition of organic matter. Over the years, these energy-rich remains were covered by layers of mud, and the matter settled into basins and oxidized while it decomposed. Heat and pressure from these layers helped the remains turn into what we today call crude oil, also referred to as a 'fossil fuel' because of its origins. Most places where crude oil is found were once sea beds. Crude is found in the interstices between sandstone and limestone or dolomite; it is found in reservoirs in sedimentary rock. Tiny pores in the rock allowed the petroleum to seep in, and these 'reservoir rocks' hold the oil like a sponge, trapped by other non-porous layers forming a sort of trap.

There are many regions in the world with different geological features that formed as the Earth's crust shifted. Some of these regions have more and larger petroleum traps. In some reservoir rock, the oil is more concentrated in pools, making it easier to extract, while in other reservoirs it is diffused throughout the rock.

The Middle East is a region that exhibits favorable characteristics - the petroleum traps are large and numerous, and the reservoir rock holds the oil in substantial pools. This region's dominance in world oil supply is the clear result. Other regions, however, also have large oil deposits, even if the oil is more difficult to identify and more expensive to extract. The United States, with its rich oil history, is such a region.

Texas has been the largest producing state since the late 1920s, when it surpassed California. For a time in the late 1980s, Alaska rivaled Texas, as the more mature Texas fields declined (and new discoveries hadn't yet been made) and production from the giant Alaskan North Slope fields, begun in 1977, was still approaching its peak level of about 2 million barrels per day. Since that time, however, production from the Alaskan North Slope has fallen rapidly.

New production areas, or "plays," led to a resurgence in activity in the Gulf of Mexico, one of the few areas with active new leasing. Leasing, drilling, production and the numbers of fields under development all set records in 1997, as the deepwater Gulf of Mexico became the place to be for almost any larger oil company, domestic or foreign. These new prospective oil producing areas are further offshore, in the much more challenging deepwater. Over one-fourth of the crude oil produced in the United States is produced offshore in the Gulf of Mexico.

What exactly is crude? It is simply unrefined petroleum.

The petroleum industry often characterizes crude oils according to their geographical source, such as West Texas Intermediate, Alaska North Slope Crude or Siberian Light. Oils from different geographical areas have unique properties. There are many types and grades of crude oil, and they vary widely in appearance and odor. Crude can be very light in color to jet black, and it can be light and thin or as thick as molasses. While all crudes are basically hydrocarbons, there are variations in molecular structure. This means specific crude can be easier or harder to extract, produce, pipeline and refine, and their properties can influence their suitability for certain end products. Much of the world's crude oil is today produced from drilled wells.

Chemists are excited about **hydrocarbons** because:

1) Hydrocarbons contain a lot of **energy**. Many of the things derived from crude oil like gasoline, diesel fuel, paraffin wax and so on take advantage of this energy.

2) Hydrocarbons **can take on many different forms**. The smallest hydrocarbon is methane (CH_4), which is a gas that is a lighter than air. Very long chains of hydrocarbons are solids like wax or tar. Hydrocarbons with five to 20 atoms in the chain produce crude; fewer than five atoms create natural gas. By chemically cross-linking hydrocarbon chains you can get everything from synthetic rubber to nylon to the plastic in tupperware. Hydrocarbon chains are very versatile.

Crudes can be roughly classified into three groups:

⊠ Light-weight components

⊠ Medium-weight components

⊠ Heavy-weight components

According to *The International Crude Oil Market Handbook*, published by the Energy Intelligence Group, there are about 161 different internationally-traded crude oils.[1] Two important crude oils which are either traded themselves or whose prices are reflected in other types of crude oil include **West Texas Intermediate** and **Brent.** These two crude oils are often compared with EIA's Imported Refiner Acquisition Cost (IRAC), the OPEC Basket, and NYMEX (New York Mercantile Exchange, where commodities are traded on a daily basis). Generally, differences in the prices of these various crude oils are related to quality differences, but other factors can also influence the price relationships between each other. Dubai-Oman crude is used as benchmark for Middle East sour crude oil flowing to the Asia-Pacific region.

The price a producer receives on his crude depends on 1) the specific grade or quality of the oil or gas, 2) the location of the well or field (access to pipelines or refineries), and 3) the number of purchasers competing.

West Texas Intermediate

West Texas Intermediate (WTI) crude oil is of very high quality and is excellent for refining a larger portion of gasoline. It is a light and sweet crude (containing only about 0.24 percent of sulfur). Combined with its location and high quality, WIT is an ideal crude oil to be refined in the United States, the largest gasoline consuming country in the world. Most WTI crude oil gets refined in the Midwest region of the country, with some more refined within the Gulf Coast region. Although the production of WTI crude oil is on the decline, it still is the major benchmark of crude oil in the Americas. WTI is generally priced at about a $5 to $6 per-barrel premium to the OPEC Basket price and about $1 to $2 per-barrel premium to Brent, although on a daily basis the pricing relationships between these can vary.

Brent

Brent Blend is actually a combination of crude oil from 15 different oil fields in the Brent and Ninian systems in the North Sea. It is light and sweet but less sweet than WTI. Brent blend is ideal for making gasoline and middle distillates, both of which are consumed in large quantities in Northwest Europe, where Brent blend crude oil is typically refined. However, if the arbitrage between Brent and other crude oils, including WTI, is favorable for export, Brent has been known to be refined in the United States (typically the East Coast or the Gulf Coast) or in the Mediterranean region. Brent blend production, like WTI, is also on the decline, but it remains the major benchmark for other crude oils in Europe or Africa. For example, prices for other crude oils in these two continents are often priced as a differential to Brent, i.e., Brent minus $0.50. Brent blend is generally priced at about a $4 per-barrel premium to the OPEC Basket price or about a $1 to $2 per-barrel discount to WTI, although on a daily basis the pricing relationships can vary.

NYMEX Futures

The NYMEX futures price for crude oil, which is reported in almost every major newspaper and financial channel in the United States, represents (on a per-barrel basis) the market-determined value of a futures contract to either buy or sell 1,000 barrels of WTI or some other light, sweet crude oil at a specified time. **What is a futures contract?** A futures contract is a promise to deliver a given quantity of a standardized commodity at a specified place, price and time in the future. Relatively few NYMEX crude oil contracts are actually executed for physical delivery. The NYMEX market, however, provides important price information to buyers and sellers of crude oil in the United States (and around the world), making WTI the benchmark for many different crude oils. The futures market is actually a mechanism designed to distribute risk among participants on different sides (or with different expectations) of the market, but not generally to supply physical volumes of oil.

While spot markets involve the trade of physical barrels of oil, futures markets are designed as a financial mechanism. While everyone in the market wishes to buy low and sell high, buyers and sellers are on opposite sides of the transaction and their risks are inherently different. Different market participants may also have varying appetite for risk, and speculators may wish to gamble that the price will move one way or another. The futures market, a zero-sum game where there is a buyer for every seller, distributes the risk among market participants according to their positions and appetites.

Prices are reported on a weekly basis by the Energy Information Administration. The ready availability of the reported prices has enhanced "price transparency" -- the ability of any market participant to assess the prevailing price level.

Hedges are also used in the futures market, to help offset profits or losses. The futures market allows anyone to "lock in" the price for future deliveries, such as heating oil prices for the winter heating season. By using this strategy of hedging, the buyer of the hedge can limit uncertainty over pricing. For instance, a marketer can offer fixed prices to customers. Some private placement sponsors even use hedges to help protect investor cash flow.

What about the hoopla over the futures market that was in the press during the summer of 2008? "Their trading might drive up prices if they were investing in stocks or real estate. But commodity investing is different," wrote Robert Samuelson. "Investors generally don't buy the physical goods, whether oil or corn. Instead, they trade "futures contracts", which are bets on future prices in, say, six months. For every trader betting on higher prices, another trader is betting on lower prices. These trades are matched. In the stock market, all investors can profit in a rising market, and all can lose in a falling market. In the futures market, one trader's gain is another's loss…the markets work because numerous financial players…can take the other side of hedgers' trades," said Robert Samuelson in a Washington Post editorial. [2]

How is oil generally sold and traded?

In fact, oil is sold under a variety of contract arrangements and in spot transactions, in addition to be traded in futures markets. Both spot markets and futures markets provide critical price information for contract markets.

A spot transaction is an agreement to sell or buy one shipment of oil under an agreed-upon price at the time of the arrangement. In a sense, says the EIA, a consumer's purchase of gasoline is a kind of spot transaction -- the consumer needed supply, found the price acceptable, and made no promise to make additional purchases. Traditionally, however, the oil industry uses the spot market to balance supply and demand. When a company temporarily has too much supply for its own needs, it will offer some for sale in the spot market. Likewise, if it needs additional volumes to meet a demand spike, or because supply is unexpectedly curtailed, it will purchase oil on a cargo-by-cargo, shipment-by-shipment basis. In recent years, the growth of "merchant refiners" has depended on spot markets. These independent refiners manufacture products not to fill their own marketing networks, but to sell the oil in third-party transactions to the highest bidder.

Prices in spot markets send a clear signal about the supply/ demand balance. Rising prices indicate that more supply is needed, and falling prices indicate that there is too much supply for the prevailing demand level. There are "spot markets" for different commodities and qualities (crude oil, for instance, as distinct from gasoline or heating oil, and low sulfur crude oil as distinct from high sulfur crude oil), and for different regions (Rotterdam/Northwest Europe, New York Harbor/ U.S. Northeast, Chicago/U.S. Midwest, Singapore/South East Asia, and the U.S. Gulf Coast, for instance). The evolution of a regional market into a pricing center has its foundation in logistics. Spot prices are reported and are relatively "transparent" -- they are reported by a number of sources and widely available in a variety of media.

The futures contracts are traded for each month for 18 months in the future, which provide a forward price curve of what to expect. Thus, the futures market also allows a mechanism for companies to profit from changes in market prices by holding nearly risk-free inventories in a rising market. Moreover, options and other well-developed over-the-counter financial mechanisms allow participants to limit their risk without eliminating their benefit in the event of higher or lower than expected prices. The mechanisms together have allowed companies to offer "price caps" and/or fixed price deals to their customers.

Contract arrangements in the oil market in fact cover most oil that changes hands. In earlier decades, contracts covered almost all oil, with terms that were infrequently readjusted. Even the pricing term of the contract was only seldom re-examined. Prices at all levels of the oil market were relatively stable. Pricing power was more dominantly in the hands of the seller, because oil availability was the paramount issue for purchasers. After the very high prices of the early 1980's, demand declined and supply increased, leading to significant price declines. At the same time, additional players (both countries and companies) entered the oil market. Worries over supply faded. It became apparent that the old constant price called for in most contracts was too high -- higher than the purchaser would pay in the abundantly-supplied open market. Purchasers rebelled, with many abandoning contracts and relying instead on the spot market. To coax them back, suppliers granted pricing terms tied to a market indicator -- the spot market, for instance, or the futures market. Thus while most oil flows under contract, its price varies with spot markets. Contract arrangements for different products are discussed below.

Most of the crude oil that flows in **international trade** is priced by formula: a base price, usually based on a market indicator, plus or minus a quality adjustment. For crude oil sold into the U.S. Gulf Coast, for instance, the base would commonly be the price of West Texas Intermediate crude oil.

Pricing over time:

Let's get a perspective on pricing here, as a potential investor. This chart is of West Texas Intermediate crude:

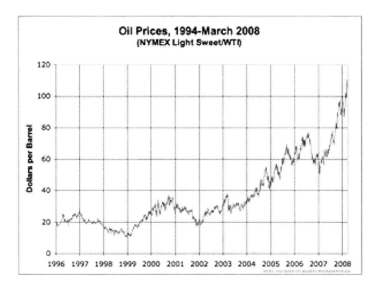

WTI/Light Sweet crude chart of daily price quotes from NYMEX, updated to March. Source http://octane.nmt.edu/gotech/ Marketplace/Prices.aspx 20 May 2008 (UTC). By permission.

Production in the United States has several unusual aspects. One is the private ownership of resource rights. In most major producing countries, the government owns the rights to develop resources. For privately owned property in the United States, the decision to explore for and produce oil is between the landowner and the producing company. The producing company compensates the landowner by the payment of a royalty on each barrel of oil produced. Early in the industry's development, there were few government restrictions. Now, there are overriding rules about well spacing and environmental standards. The only government agency to restrict production volume was the Texas Railroad Commission, which limited production in Texas depending on projected demand and production volumes in other areas of the United States. However, since the early 1970s, there have been no restrictions to production by any government agency.

The private ownership of resource rights contributes to two other aspects unique to production in the United States -- the active participation of thousands of independent producers and the prevalence of the "stripper" well, one producing less than 10 barrels a day. As the industry was developing, many entrepreneurs with limited capital resources, but a high tolerance for risk, joined its ranks and, in fact, discovered some of the largest fields in the United States. Most of the time, their finds were less dramatic, but large enough for a small company to be a success. The company's success was, of course, the landowner's success as well. Many of the wells never flowed with very high volume and, as they aged, volume dropped. Nonetheless, stripper wells are likely to remain in production as long as the price of oil covers the production cost. They currently account for about 75 percent of all wells in production in the United States and produce somewhat less than 900,000 barrels per day, 15 percent of the total U.S. crude oil production.

What is refined and taken out of one barrel of Oil?

Let's understand what comes from each barrel of gas, so that you understand as an investor how this plays out. Keep in mind that as the grade and type of crude will vary, so will what is refined from it:

One Barrel (42 Gal.) of Oil Yields:

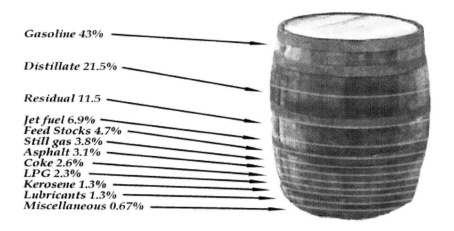

Gasoline 43%

Distillate 21.5%

Residual 11.5

Jet fuel 6.9%
Feed Stocks 4.7%
Still gas 3.8%
Asphalt 3.1%
Coke 2.6%
LPG 2.3%
Kerosene 1.3%
Lubricants 1.3%
Miscellaneous 0.67%

Courtesy of Maverick Energy (maverickenergy.com)

We know that the most common products from petroleum are energy products: gasoline, heating oil, and diesel fuel. However, items such as ink, crayons, bubble gum, dishwashing liquids, telephones, linoleum, floor wax, deodorant, eyeglasses, soft contact lenses, aspirin, tires, footballs, milk jugs and heart valves are also made from petroleum.

WHAT ABOUT NATURAL GAS?

Oil gets all of the attention – it is sexy and expensive and contentious and snatches the headlines. Natural gas is the quiet cousin. Natural gas is believed by many to be one of more important energy sources short-term. Existing supplies worldwide as well as domestically, coupled with more environmental soundness and multiple applications across sectors, means that natural gas can play a role. But remember, it is a depleting asset and like oil, there is an ultimate finite supply. So the excitement is mixed.

Natural gas offers certain advantages over other fossil fuels: a relatively low greenhouse signature, energy efficiency and ease of use. The nature of the natural gas market is similar to other competitive commodity markets: prices reflect the ability of supply to meet demand at any one time. Like any other commodity, the price of natural gas is largely a function of demand and the supply of the product.

We often think of natural gas as primarily a fuel for heating and cooking, but it is also used widely for electric power generation (and is taking over for coal), in industrial processes and for petrochemical manufacturing.

According to the EIA, natural gas accounts for 22% of the world energy mix and demand is growing, particularly in the electricity sector in OECD countries. In its "Annual Energy Outlook 2004", the EIA predicted a 1.5% annual increases in demand over the next 21 years. It accounts for only 3% demand in the transportation section, but is expected to increase. Different federal agencies and groups have made varying predictions, but they all say that a steady increase in demand is certain. Increasingly, environmental policies favor the use of relatively cleaner natural gas over other fossil fuels. At the same time, high oil prices have stimulated the rise of new sources of gas demand, as oil producers use natural gas to produce very heavy oil.

The EIA predicts the demand for electricity to increase 1.8% annually to 2025. Natural gas has been growing (over coal) as an energy used to generate electricity – it is cleaner than coal and there is a lower capital requirement (and shorter construction times) for building natural gas generation plants. In 2002, natural gas accounted for 16% of electricity generation. The EIA estimates 57% of all new electric-generation plants built by 2025 will be using natural gas or natural gas in combination with other sources. Increased demand for electricity combined with retirement of old nuclear, petroleum and coal generation plans leaves room for natural gas to step in.

THE EIA gives us the following statistics about our domestic natural gas industry:

Producers - There are over 6,300 producers of natural gas in the United States. These companies range from large integrated producers with worldwide operations and interests in all segments of the oil and gas industry, to small one or two person operations that may only have partial interest in a single well. The largest integrated production companies are termed 'Majors', of which 21 are active

Processing - There are over 530 natural gas processing plants in the United States.

Pipelines - There are about 160 pipeline companies in the U.S., operating over 300,000 miles of pipe.

Storage - There are about 123 natural gas storage operators in the U.S., which control approximately 400 underground storage facilities. They are found everywhere but concentrated in the northeast.

Marketers - As of 2000, there were over 260 companies involved in the marketing of natural gas. In this same year, about 80 percent of all the natural gas supplied and consumed in North America passed through the hands of natural gas marketers.

Local Distribution Companies - There are about 1,200 natural gas distribution companies in the U.S.

Natural gas, often informally referred to as simply "gas", is extracted from underground reservoirs, and is composed primarily of methane, along with other hydrocarbons such as ethane, propane, butane and inert gases such as carbon dioxide, nitrogen and helium. **Natural gas** is one of the three fossil fuels -- the other two are oil and coal. Oil and natural gas are produced by the same geological process: anaerobic decay of organic matter deep under the Earth's surface. As a consequence, oil and natural gas are often found together. In common usage, deposits rich in oil are known as oil fields, and deposits rich in natural gas are called natural gas fields. Oil and gas prices do not always move in tandem though both are moving up in pricing. (**Investors may consider programs that have a combination**

of oil and gas production for some diversity, or one of each to offset each a little).

Because both oil and natural gas are lighter than water, they tend to rise from their sources until they either seep to the surface or are trapped by a non-permeable layer of rock. They are extracted by drilling. Deposits of natural gas lie throughout the United States, and the most prolific production areas are in the Gulf of Mexico and the western and southwestern states

The world's large reserves of natural gas are concentrated in three countries: Russia, Iran and Qatar, with an estimated 58% of all supply there. However, the industry is far more advanced in older producing countries, like the U.S. and Canada. The U.S. has 3% (204 trillion cubic feet) of the estimated world reserves, sourced from Oil & Gas Journal, Jan 2007 as reported by EIA. The United States is one of the world's largest producers and consumers of natural gas, though our transportation sector consumes only three percent of our natural gas. Legendary oil investor T. Boone Pickens said that he sees a future in the idea of transforming some of the gas reserves into liquid motor fuels to help provide a temporary bridge to the future.

Most of the natural gas consumed in the United States comes from domestic production – we import only about 19% of the total used, according to the EIA. Our natural gas imports come from pipeline from Canada and Mexico and some liquefied natural gas from elsewhere. The United States produced 18.5 trillion cubic feet of dry natural gas in 2006, up slightly from 2005. The Federal Offshore Gulf of Mexico and five States accounted for the majority of the natural gas production in the United States, comprising 76.6 percent of the total in 2006:

- ☒ Texas (27.8 percent)
- ☒ Federal Offshore Gulf of Mexico (15.7 percent)
- ☒ Wyoming (9.4 percent)
- ☒ Oklahoma (8.6 percent)
- ☒ New Mexico (8.1 percent)

☒ Louisiana (6.8 percent)

The Barnett Shale in north Texas is one of the most active natural gas fields in North America and one of the largest, spanning 7 million acres from Dallas to Fort Worth and south. It produces about 2 billion cubic feet of gas per day. The Barnett Shale is a geological formation of economic significance consisting of sedimentary rocks (Mississippian age (354-323 million years ago)). Some experts have suggested the Barnett Shale may be the largest onshore natural gas field in the United States. Oil also has been found in lesser quantities, but sufficient enough (with recent high oil prices) to be commercially viable.

The Barnett Shale is known as a "tight" gas reservoir, indicating that the gas is not easily extracted. The shale is very hard, and it was virtually impossible to produce gas in commercial quantities from this formation until recent improvements were made in hydraulic fracturing ("fracing") technology and horizontal drilling - and of course an upturn in the natural gas price. To coax gas out of the concrete-like Barnett Shale, operators pump large amounts of water down their wells to fracture the rock. One horizontal could use about 3 million gallons of water. (Most of the water for these so-called "frac jobs" comes from groundwater). Sometimes called "Father of the Barnett Shale", George Mitchell had been drilling in the area at shallower depths for years and worked hard testing various techniques. "It took George Mitchell 18 years to make it work," notes Larry Brogdon, partner and chief geologist for Four Sevens Oil Company. "He was tenacious. He started in 1981 and it really didn't take off until 1999. " [3]

About the only thing more exciting than watching the impressive success of the Barnett Shale is watching another shale play begin to take off, say many experts. That is the case with the Woodford Shale play unfolding in southeastern Oklahoma. "The Woodford Shale is a result of what happened in the Barnett Shale of the Fort Worth Basin," Terry said. "The same type of technology has been utilized to exploit the Woodford Shale," says Mike Terry, president of the Oklahoma Independent Petroleum Association. [4] Oil giant BP announced on July 18, 2008 that is was to pay $1.75 billion to Chesapeake Oil for natural gas assets in Oklahoma, moving away from their traditional emphasis on oil. This includes the Woodford Shale.[5]

More recently, Terry Englander, a geo-science professor at Pennsylvania State University, and Gary Lash, a geology professor at the State University of New York at Fredonia, surprised everyone with estimates on the Marcellus Shale. This Shale stretches beneath much of Ohio, West Virginia, Pennsylvania and New York with small areas of Maryland, Kentucky, Tennessee, and Virginia included. They are using some of the same horizontal drilling and fracturing methods that had previously been applied in the Barnett Shale.

World production of dry natural gas was dominated by the United States (18.1 Tcf) and Russia (22.6 Tcf), whose combined gross production accounts for about 40 percent produced in 2005. Many do believe that gas production peaked in North America in 2002, and it has been declining ever since (about 1.7% annually), even though there has been a tripling of production.[6] J. David Hughes, a research geologist with the Geological Survey of Canada and an expert on North American natural gas, was quoted in *Profit from the Peak* to explain the trend: "U.S. gas production peaked in about the second quarter of 2001 and has been going down or remaining flat since that time. Canada's gas production hit a plateau in mid-2001 and maintained that plateau until mid-2002. And then, despite drilling a record number of holes, production went down about three and a half percent. We drilled another record number of holes in 2004, and production stayed pretty much flat. So you've got no production response to all that extra drilling." [7]

Let's take a look at Natural Gas prices since 1999, courtesy of EIA:

Table 5c. U.S. Regional Natural Gas Prices
Dollars per Thousand Cubic Feet

	1999	2000	2001	2002	2003	2004	2005	2006	2007	2008	2009
Wholesale/Spot											
U.S. Average											
Wellhead	2.19	3.7	4.01	2.95	4.89	5.45	7.26	6.4	6.39	9.82	9.96
Henry Hub Spot Price	2.34	4.44	4.08	3.46	5.64	6.08	8.94	6.94	7.17	11.05	10.99
Residential											
New England	9.48	10.22	12.55	10.49	12.43	14.15	15.49	17.55	16.5	18.28	20.58
Middle Atlantic	8.47	8.84	10.62	9.06	11.19	12.2	13.54	15.64	15.01	17.07	19.08
East North Central	5.7	6.8	8.38	6.89	8.57	9.55	11.76	12.38	11.62	13.69	15.57
West North Central	5.88	7.42	9.26	7.06	8.84	10.11	11.85	12.57	12.04	13.53	15.95
South Atlantic	8.22	9.36	11.35	9.81	11.59	13.09	15.61	17.18	16.45	18.13	20.29
East South Central	6.61	7.85	10.47	8.46	10.01	11.34	13.87	15.48	14.12	15.71	18.19
West South Central	6.3	7.54	9.35	7.66	9.42	10.6	12.56	13.46	12.35	14.64	17.02
Mountain	5.87	6.54	8.49	7.01	7.75	9.18	10.9	12.02	10.93	12.88	14.94
Pacific	6.51	7.98	10.15	7.52	8.98	9.81	11.75	12.02	11.98	14.15	15.73
U.S. Average	**6.69**	**7.77**	**9.63**	**7.9**	**9.63**	**10.75**	**12.7**	**13.75**	**13**	**14.84**	**16.92**

Just a few words about liquid natural gas (LNG): While natural gas as a primary fuel is expected to grow at 3 percent per year during the next two decades, LNG is expected to grow at double that rate for the same time period. **What is LNG?** Natural gas which has been liquefied by reducing its temperature to minus 260 degrees Fahrenheit at atmospheric pressure. "Given the enormity of our energy needs, a segment of our supply has to come from LNG," says former U.S. Representative Philip Sharp, who served as Congressional chair of the National Commission on Energy Policy and is now president of Resources for the Future, an environmental think tank in Washington, D.C. "There's no way that cleaner sources add up to what we need, and gas is much cleaner than coal or oil. LNG should not become an excuse for failing to press forward on energy efficiency and renewable fuels, but we have to deal within the confines of our political and economic institutions…" says Sharp. [8]

Advantages of Natural Gas

1) Advantages of natural gas include that it can be used directly as it is taken from the ground, while other fuels must be refined. However, it is cleaned, purified and an odorant is added for safety measures, as it is nearly odorless once purified. 2) It is a cleaner fuel. It has an octane rating of about 130 as compared to 90 for gasoline and costs less on a per-gallon equivalent basis than gasoline or diesel. Natural gas vehicles generally burn 80 percent cleaner than conventional vehicles. Natural gas leads to reduced engine maintenance and to longer engine life. 3) It may play an important role in electricity generation. 4) The U.S. has good fields of natural gas, which could help alleviate dependence from abroad, at least for some time.

Disadvantages also exist.

1) Natural gas occupies about four times the space of an energy equivalent of gasoline resulting in added weight and space of fuel storage tanks. New fuel tanks and some fuel system modifications are required on retrofits. At the present time, there is limited availability of refueling stations and natural gas vehicles experience a shorter driving range between fill-ups. 2) Unlike some products where production can

be increased quickly, increases in natural gas production need longer lead times. It takes time to acquire leases, secure required government permits, do exploratory seismic work, drill wells and connect wells to pipelines; this can take as little as 6 months, and in some cases up to ten years. 3) When natural gas wells start to deplete, they do so immediately, like falling off a cliff. This is unlike oil wells, whereby there is usually a gradual decline. Investors need to know this. 4) And while there are good reserves of natural gas today, it is not a renewable energy (like solar or wind) and it is a fossil fuel, albeit it a much cleaner fossil fuel than its counterparts. Fossil fuels will run out.

Keep in mind, global factors also can have an impact on natural gas, though theoretically not as much as oil. An example: Japan had an earthquake last year, disabling a crucial nuclear plant. To make up for lost power, the country turned to natural gas. To entice tankers of gas their way, they offered higher prices. "On a global scale, now you're competing with other countries who may be willing to pay more," says Sasha Weintraub, at Progress Energy. [9] Here is another factor: hurricanes can affect the work on extracting and shipping natural gas, and demand may go up after the storm, storage supplies go down while new supply is disrupted, all which creates a spike in prices.

However, looking at the advantages and disadvantages to natural gas found within our borders, it could indeed be one of a number of fuels that could help ease our dependence on imported oil for the near future.

Let's Talk About Drilling and Extracting Oil and Gas

The process of getting crude oil and natural gas out of the ground, and to its final destination, is not simple. The practice of locating oil and gas and deposits has been transformed dramatically in the last 15 years with extremely advanced and sophisticated technology. In the early days of the industry, the only way of locating underground petroleum and natural gas deposits was to search for surface evidence of these underground formations. Those searching for natural gas deposits were forced to scour the earth, looking for seepages of oil or gas emitted from underground before they had any clue that there were deposits underneath. However, because such a low proportion of petroleum and natural gas deposits actually seep to the surface, this made for a very inefficient and difficult exploration process.

Historically, drilling a "wildcat" well -- searching for oil in a field where it had not yet been discovered -- had a low chance of success. Only one out of five wildcat wells found oil or gas. Better information, especially from seismic technology, has improved the success rate to one out of three and, according to some, one in two. New drilling technologies including satellites, global positioning systems, remote sensing devices, and 3-D and 4-D seismic technologies make it possible to discover oil reserves while drilling fewer wells.

Finding and extracting petroleum isn't a single activity. It is a series of steps: identifying a prospective area through various studies, gaining the lease rights or ownership, getting permits, assembling teams, overseeing drilling and field teams, leasing or buying drilling rigs and all of the equipment, casing, pipes, mud and cement necessary, getting access to water, perhaps building a road, testing the rock, doing the actual drilling, determining whether the find is commercially viable and estimating the dimensions of the reservoir with further drilling. Production wells are then installed and gathering pipelines assembled to transport it to central points.

Prospective sites are identified using 3-D, seismic testing (with return vibrations), analyzing of nearby wells (if there are any), and by using techniques such as core sampling -- physically removing and testing a cross section of the rock. After these analysis and initial tests, companies must then drill to confirm the presence of oil or gas. A "dry hole" is an unsuccessful well, one where the drilling did not find oil or gas, or not enough to be economically worth producing. A successful well may contain either oil or gas, and often both, because the gas is dissolved in the oil.

When a successful well identifies the presence of oil and/or gas, additional wells are drilled to test the production conditions and determine the boundaries of the reservoir. Drilling an exploratory well can average 2 to 6 months. Drilling depths, rock hardness, weather conditions and other factors all have an affect on the time necessary for drilling. Finally, production, or "development," wells are put in place, along with tanks, pumps, pipelines and such, so the crude can be produced, moved to markets and sold.

The naturally occurring pressure in the underground reservoir is an important facet in determining whether the reservoir is economically viable or not. The pressure varies with the characteristics of the trap, the reservoir rock and the production history. Most oil, initially, is produced by "natural lift" production methods: the pressure underground is high enough to force the oil to the surface. (Reservoirs in the Middle East tend to be long-lived on "natural lift," that is, the reservoir pressure continues over time to be great enough to force the oil out.) The underground pressure in older reservoirs will eventually dissipate, and oil no longer flows to the surface naturally. It must be pumped out by means of an "artificial lift" -- a pump powered by gas or electricity. The majority of the oil reservoirs in the United States use some kind of artificial lift. Investors need to understand - over time, these production methods become ineffective, and continued production requires the use of additional "secondary" production methods. A frequently used method uses water to displace oil ("waterflood"), to force the oil to the drilled shaft. Producers may eventually need to turn to "tertiary" methods, which usually are centered on increasing the oil's flow through the use of steam, carbon dioxide and other gases or chemicals. In the United States, primary production methods account for about 40 percent of the oil produced on a daily basis, secondary methods account for about half, and tertiary recovery the remaining 10 percent.

The reservoir characteristics and the physical characteristics of the crude oil are important components of the costs. Costs can range from as little as $2 per barrel in the Middle East to $15 per barrel and more in some fields in the United States (this includes capital recovery). Technological advances in finding and producing oil have made it possible to bring once-expensive deepwater Gulf of Mexico oil into production at a reasonable cost. However, "exploration costs" can vary dramatically. The cost for unsuccessful exploration, which consists of seismic studies and a dry well, can cost $5 million to $20 million per exploration site, and in some cases, much more.[9] I address more about the cost of drilling in Chapter 6.

In gas production and development, production and condensation plants are required in which a liquification plant provides treatment, refrigeration and liquification followed by the storage and loading of liquefied gas. The gas is transferred to liquefied natural gas tankers (LNG's) which transports it to a treatment plant where a "re-gasification" process occurs.

In its raw state, crude oil is transported by two primary modes: tankers, which travel interregional water routes, and pipelines where most of the oil moves through for at least part of the route. Today's tanker vessels, which include both ships and barges, are responsible for moving of the vast volumes of liquid cargoes.

The transportation and storage industry is a very complex system in itself, with many independent owners. For example, the tanker transportation industry is a very fragmented industry with 75 percent of the world tanker fleet being independently owned. In the natural gas transport and storage network, nearly all is transported through interstate pipelines owned by at least 70 to 80 companies to over several hundred underground storage facilities.

Just as oil resources are not evenly distributed around the globe, neither are they evenly distributed throughout the United States. Given the way production data are reported, the biggest production region by far is the U.S. Gulf Coast, and the largest producing state is Texas. The Gulf Coast region is home to two of the most important producing provinces, the Permian Basin, located inland in West Central Texas and Eastern New Mexico, and the Federal Offshore portion of the Gulf of Mexico.

Some investors have asked in the past– if prices drop, would wells be turned off? There are several economic drivers that provide incentives to continue producing even in the face of lower prices.

- If production is halted from a natural gas well it may not be possible to restore the well's production due to reservoir and wellbore characteristics.

- If a producer chooses not to operate a well, the lost production cannot be recovered the next month but is instead is deferred potentially years in the future.

- Related specifically to gas: Some gas is produced in association with oil, and in order to stop the flow of natural gas, the oil production must be stopped as well, which may not be economic.

- A producer may be financially or contractually bound to produce.

- As we have seen in this book, the supply and demand factors are entrenched.

*The London-based Oil Depletion Analysis Centre recently released
a study that predicted tight supplies through the rest of this decade,
even if all of the new major oil recovery projects scheduled to come on stream
over the next six years meet their targets. The only way to avoid it, the study
said, is for demand to drop sharply. 2008*

*We have long had death and taxes as the two standards of inevitability.
But there are those who believe that death is the preferable of the two.
"At least," as one man said, "there's one advantage about death; it doesn't get
worse every time Congress meets." Erwin N. Griswold*

Taxation with *representation ain't so hot either.* Gerald Barzan

CHAPTER 5:
TAX BENEFITS

The author is not a tax attorney or CPA. This chapter discusses the commonly known tax benefits as they are in the tax code today, and is intended to help inform potential investors. The specific program offering will detail the kind of tax benefits
to expect. Any potential investor should always review their specific and personal situation with their accountant or attorney! Remember that the tax code and laws can change.

Judge Learned Hand (1872- 1961), considered to be one of the most influential American judges and an intellectual leader, is famous for the following quote:

"Anyone may arrange his affairs so that his taxes shall be as low as possible; he is not bound to choose that pattern which best pays the treasury. There is not even a patriotic duty to increase one's taxes. Over and over again the Courts have said that there is nothing sinister in so arranging affairs as to keep taxes as low as possible. Everyone does it, rich and poor alike and all do right, for nobody owes any public duty to pay more than the law demands."[1]

When it comes to tax-advantaged investments for accredited investors, one investment class continues to stand alone above all others: Oil and Gas. This includes AMT preference exclusions, "active" rather than "passive" write offs, high tax write-offs from drilling programs, and tax shelters on the income from oil and gas. With the backing of the U.S. government, an array of tax incentives were placed into the tax code to help encourage domestic production. The kind of oil and gas program that you invest in will dictate the kind of tax benefits you will get. For instance, in a pure drilling program, you could gain 75% to 100% of your investment dollars as a write-off in the year of investment (depending on the structure of the program). The cash flow from drilling, working interest or re-work programs will then have an annual 15% depletion allowance or sheltering. Royalty programs normally are allowed the 15% depletion allowance on the royalties you are paid, but none of the other benefits. However, some royalty programs may work for the 1031 tax deferred exchange, which can be another tax advantage. By the way, a few working interest programs are also structured for the 1031 though they may not be 100% compliant and would not fulfill the debt side of a 1031 requirement as they are not generally leveraged.

"Tax-advantaged" refers to the economic bonus which applies to certain accounts or investments that are, by statute, tax-reduced, tax-deferred, or tax-free. The most obvious examples are retirement plans, but investments in municipal bonds can also be exempt from certain taxes, for example. Governments establish the tax-advantaged status to encourage private individuals to invest money when it is considered to be in the public interest. A "Tax shelter" is an investment vehicle designed to protect or shelter investor income from federal taxation, and tax shelters are legally available, including with oil and gas investments. There are, in fact, several major tax benefits available for oil and gas investors that are found nowhere else in the tax code. The drilling programs are the most beneficial for investors.

A summary of benefits are listed below. **These types of benefits are obviously not available to those purchasing stock in publicly-traded oil companies, or mutual funds, and illustrates one of the benefits of a DPP investment.**

TAX INCENTIVES

Intangible Drilling Costs (IDCs). Typically all costs incurred in drilling that have no salvage value. IDCs are the intangible drilling expenses incidental to and necessary for the drilling of a well, such as the labor, surveying, grease, chemicals, consumable supplies, installation costs, etc. IDCs are usually about 65% to 80%++ of the overall drilling costs and are written off.

Tangible Drilling Costs are 100% tax deductible, and is the amount allocated to the tangible equipment.

Leasing Costs (purchase of leases, mineral rights, etc.), legal expenses, administrative accounting and lease operating costs are all deductible.

"Percentage Depletion Allowance". The 1990 Tax Act provided special tax advantages for small companies and individuals not available to large oil companies, retail marketers or refiners. This is a tax free allowance of 15% of the annual gross income from oil and gas. (A second choice, called cost depletion, is also an option though most seem to choose percentage depletion). Percentage depletion is similar to depreciation in real estate. Depletion is defined as the exhaustion of the mineral deposit through its extraction. The depletion allowance is applied to the drilling, working interest and rework programs, through programs whereby oil or gas being is being extracted and sold.

By the way, cost depletion for any year is determined by dividing the tax basis of a property by the estimated total barrels of oil (or MCF for gas) recoverable, and then multiplying the per-unit allowance by the number of units sold during the year. It cannot exceed the adjusted tax basis of the property. Most investors tend to use percentage depletion (15%).

Active vs. Passive Income: The Tax Code specifically states that a **Working Interest in oil and gas is not passive, so deductions can be offset against income from stock trades, business income, salaries** and such (Section 469(c)(3) of the Tax Code), on Schedule C. That is, IF the taxpayer's interest is owned directly or through an entity that does not limit the taxpayer's liability with respect to drilling operations. It should be noted that if an investor uses an S Corporation, limited partnership or a trust, the working interest exception will not apply to the shareholder, limited partner or beneficiary because that form of ownership limits the liability. Not all oil and gas investments involve a Working Interest, but if it does, you may offset active income with the deductions.

Alternative Minimum Tax – Exempted Tax Preference Items
Since the 1992 Tax Act, Intangible Drilling Costs were specifically exempted as a tax preference item. Alternative Minimum Taxable Income generally consists of the adjusted gross income minus allowable items plus the sum of tax preference items. Included in this are deductions for intangible drilling and development costs as well as the deduction for depletion.

The Sponsor (the company that handles the offering and is in charge of the venture) will supply each investor the necessary documentation for their accountant. In general, this is in the form of a K-1, but if not a partnership, documentation is provided so that your percentage interest can easily be calculated.

Investors who are comfortable with the drilling programs (no immediate income) typically want or need tax benefits in the year of investment. They then build cash flow in subsequent year as the wells come online. Some investors, myself included, have been using a "laddering" system. That is, each year, we invest in a drilling program to benefit from tax advantages for that year, and each subsequent year our cash flow is building from those investments. I would encourage that you consult your accountant on any of the tax aspects and how they may help or affect you.

Some investors are pleased over the Active vs. Passive write-downs available; others need assistance on AMT preference items and are thrilled that they have this choice. Some investors are looking to bump up the actual cash flow from their real estate returns or other more conservative holdings like bonds, while others who are disappointed in their mutual fund or stock performances and are willing to take on a little risk put some monies to work into an oil and gas program, while gaining the tax benefits at the same time.

The United States Oil and Gas Corp gives the following scenario: Suppose you invest $25,000 in a drilling deal this year. Say you get to deduct $18,000 from your 2008 income (the write off allowed through the drilling deductions of the program you chose). In a 39.6% federal tax bracket, that deduction would save you more than $7,000 in tax payments. [2]

As explained in the *Oil & Gas Federal Income Taxation 2007* guide, taxation of natural resources is one of the more complicated areas of the tax system. The rules are based on certain concepts not found in other areas of taxation.[3] Most investors will want to confer with their accountants and give them lead time to fully investigate all of the benefits and write-offs that will be due to you.

Please: Always review your specific and personal situation with your CPA as regards the various tax benefits, and what may benefit you!

*"There is irony about depleting a finite resource: the better you
are at doing the job, the sooner it ends."
Colin Campbell, Chair, ASPO (Association for the Study
of Peak Oil). April 2006, Solar Today Newsletter.*

*"..the American people are so "dumbed down" by television that they have
little or no awareness of what is happening to them. The media have
been engulfed by corporate mergers...The result? For years, studies such as
those by University of Massachusetts Center for Studies in Communication,
have shown that people who get their news primarily from television are
not only poorly informed, but often seriously misinformed"
Richard Heinberg, in his book PowerDown. 2004*

"If a little money does not go out, great money will not come in."
Confucius (551BC - 479BC) philosopher

CHAPTER 6:
TYPES OF INVESTMENT PROGRAMS

What are some of the typical investment programs?

* I. Drilling Programs

This could include Developmental Drilling (recommended), Exploratory Drilling (non recommended) or a combination of both. The programs are structured to encompass the full pre- to post-drilling and completion process, and then operation of the wells, with income flowing from the sale of petroleum.

Tax benefits are a draw, with 70% to 99% of investment dollar write-offs possible.

* II. Working Interest Income Programs

These are programs whereby the wells are already drilled and cash flow is in place from working, producing wells. Acquisition of working and operating wells. Cash flow in place is the draw here, and depletion is allowed to shelter some of that income.

* III. Combination of Income Program and new Drilling

For investors who want some tax benefits derived from drilling, but also want some current cash flow from working wells. The overall age of the income offering will be somewhat extended due to the age of the newly drilled wells.

* IV. Rework Programs

Reworks (updating and repair of operating or stripper wells) may be offered alone on a group of wells or in combination with programs mentioned above.

* V. Royalty Programs

Royalties are the monies received by the land owner in return for allowing drilling and operation of wells on his land. In these programs, an overriding royalty is paid to the investors, with no other specific involvement or benefits from drilling or working interests except for depletion in some cases. More conservative investment.

* VI. There are also some **Note or Debenture** programs whose underlying collateral is oil and gas; there are some **private placement structures** that pay specific and steady income and whose underlying business is oil and gas.

I like the following quotes from Thomas Brown, made in 1981 but which still rings true today, "There are good, bad, indifferent, great, terrible and crooked deals…A good deal can be broadly defined as one that is in a clear and acceptable format and provides reasonable economics and an accurate appraisal of risk…Oil deals will continue to be constructed, explained, argued over, bought, sold, rejected, modified and laughed at as long as the economic incentives exist to warrant the search for oil and gas. Participants in these ventures will experience agony, ecstasy, frustration, wealth and occasional heartburn…"[1]

I. DRILLING PROGRAMS

The most popular oil and gas DPP investment choice by far is the Drilling Program. Why? Generous tax benefits and the potential subsequent high cash flows. Drilling programs are often chosen by investors who immediately want a tax write off (in the year of investment), and who would like to see some good potential cash flow bumps to their portfolio in subsequent years (after the wells are drilled and are producing). The tax benefits can be quite beneficial – 75% to 100% of the investment dollars can be written off, as we have reviewed on the chapter about tax benefits. With the price of oil and gas and demand for it, the cash flow in the following years can be advantageous, too.

The program sponsor is usually an oil company who structures the deal. They are usually involved in the drilling, oversight and management of the offerings, or they may hire or joint-venture with an operating and drilling company and oversee the offering. Sometimes in offerings with numerous locations and sites, the sponsor may engage several operators or teams found in the various locations. Drilling programs are often structured so that the investor can come in as a general partner (and gain the highest write-offs, though with some liability) or they can invest immediately as a limited partner (and gain write-offs but not as high). Apart from General or Limited Partnerships, other structures seen are Limited Liability Company (LLC) structure, joint-ventures, direct ownerships, etc. In fact, there are many ways to structure a deal. The Private Placement Memorandum (PPM) will always explain the structure and details.

The common theme, no matter the structure, is that the sponsor raises money from the investors to fund the drilling of the wells (from start to finish), and whose goal is to make money for the investors on the extraction and sale of petroleum from those drilled wells.

As a rule of thumb, if you invest in a new Drilling Program, **you will not receive any income for 6 months to a year, while the wells are being drilled and brought online**. This will depend on the type of program you choose, where it is and the drilling schedule - if you are getting in after drilling has started or not, for instance. In exchange, you are able to gain that big tax write-off in year one. Thereafter, from year 2, you will be able to claim depletion on the income generated from the wells (typically 15%). The tax code allows an oil company to drill no later than March of the year following the investment for them to count (i.e. a drilling program with 20 wells offered in 2007 drilled 15 by December 31 but drilled the remaining 5 wells before March 2008, so they all counted for 2007 write-offs).

Offering sponsors report that a large part of the equity invested into their drilling programs comes in the 4th quarter as investors are planning their taxes. However, drilling programs are available all year. I have some investors who put a small amount into a program early in the year, especially if the drilling schedule is immediate, and invest into another deal in the 4th quarter with the amount that makes sense for their total tax-planning purposes. This moves up some of the cash flow from the earlier program –as those wells come on line earlier- while gaining the tax benefits they want or need for the year. It also gives diversity.

Drilling programs, as mentioned previously, are for investors who are not risk adverse. Technology is far better today in the oil and gas industry, and more efficient that it was, and this helps reduce some drilling risk. However, depending on the program, the sponsor, their experience, where the drilling shall occur, etc., they could hit a dry hole or drill a well where pressure is low and ineffectual, run into problems in the field due to shortages of equipment or teams, have a hurricane or severe weather to cause delays, or other myriad details that affect extraction of the oil. I generally like programs that offer a number of wells, perhaps in various sites – but never just one or a few wells in one area. I also prefer hands-down the proven and trusted sponsors.

What Should I Review? What is important in a Drilling Program?

I recommend two overriding factors when it comes to an investment choice:

1) The sponsor
2) The proposed program and its objectives.

The sponsor is in fact extremely important here. Their success will be your success; they must bring expertise, devotion, transparency, care and professionalism to the venture. You must get a comfort level with the sponsor before you invest. They must know what they are doing on the ground and/or in overseeing the process. They should have some "skin in the game" (i.e. investment in the project, for instance). They must have good legal to make sure title is clear and leases are secured properly. They must have smart geologists and/or geophysicists. They must have good access to (or own) the rigs and equipment necessary to accomplish the goals. They must be capitalized and able to pay bills, secure bonds, pay for insurance and handle surprises. They must be good managers. They must know how to come in on budget and manage the multiple facets to the entire program. As mentioned, sometimes the sponsor will team up with a drilling company or another oil & gas company, sometimes they do the work themselves and sometimes they engage and oversee teams to do the work. They must have field contacts, field experience and 'savvy'.

Always refer to the Private Placement Memorandum (PPM) or offering document, which will explain **where** the drilling will occur, the **objectives**, the **amount of the offering** and number of units to be offered, **how** those investor funds will be used, **what** percentage of carried interest (if any) will be held by the sponsor or any special sharing arrangement, sponsor experience and track record, **background** on the principals of the sponsor, what **fees** the sponsor will receive, the **amount of the royalty** to be paid to the landowner (before you are paid), what **commission** your registered rep will receive, **management** of the operations, and **risk factors** to consider.

Keep in mind that a **track record** isn't a substitute for review of each program the sponsor brings out, but the track record is a good demonstration of how they have managed their offerings and business. Integrity is key. When looking at the track record on all previous drilling programs, you should see the following: what is their success rate, how many dry holes, what kinds of average returns have their offerings had, what returns are more recent programs making (are they high or if low, why?), how many older programs have succeeded at full payout of investment, how often did they meet their goals in drilling schedules and such. How long have they been in the oil and gas business? How do they communicate during the investigative process before investing? Are they available to investors or have an investor relations person? Do they have regular communications with investors (newsletters or conference calls, for instance) and/or a password protected website? Do they supply reports on the well production with your monthly checks? Look for sponsors who have made a substantial investment of time and money to enter the business, and have not only acquisition and sales people, but due diligence, asset management, financial reporting, and investor relations personnel. You must know who you're doing business with.

Why is this important? When oil prices are high, more and more people enter the oil business and start assembling and marketing these deals. You want a good investment and not one with a marginal player that will result in heartache. Almost every expert, oil man, investor or registered representative will say the same thing: deal with experienced companies who are known, trusted and transparent.

In addition to knowing the sponsor, **it is important to understand the structure of the program and its objectives**. Important questions include: Who gets what percent of the revenue over the life of the project? Does the overall plan seem feasible, how will your money be used, and what are the projected returns? Compare programs. Sponsors normally provide various 'sensitivity studies' or proformas to show the various market prices of oil and/or gas and the anticipated or projected cash flows from those prices based on the amount of oil or gas expected to be extracted from the wells. In developmental program (meaning proven wells and reserves are on the sites), there is a good idea of the amount of flow to expect but it is never exact or known until drilling is complete. Are off-set wells planned and how many? (Remember, developmental means drilling in known areas of production as opposed to experimental drilling or wildcatting; Offset wells are new well locations adjoining another producing well site).

The sponsor will have outlined the general or specific areas targeted for the offering and the number of wells (or range) that they plan to drill (i.e. 10-11 wells in the Permian Basin and 10 wells in the Barnett Shale). They will have done their homework on the land they own or have tied up with leases, and the geologists and engineers will have analyzed the early data, and they continue to analyze even during drilling (reviewing various levels and depths of where the oil may be and taking the procedure through to completion). They will be key in where to drill, how deep, how to handle the problems, and how to make the hole a success. Though the science and techniques have come a long way, finding the best zone for oil is still somewhat of an art. Does the sponsor have experience in the targeted areas? Who are the geologists and how much experience do they have?

How long is the **anticipated 'payout'**, that is, the estimated amount of time to theoretically get a return of your capital? These payout estimations are tricky at best – it will depend on the market price of the oil and gas being steady or better than the proforma, that all wells hit and all are producing normally or above average, and are drilled on schedule. All of those factors are unknown at time of investment into a drilling deal. I would in general like to see an estimated payout in about 3 years (maybe 4) for oil, though some programs may actually pay out in 2 years. Brad Updike (JD, LLC, CSA), a due diligence officer at Mick & Associates says that some reputable Appalachian-based programs have come in more at perhaps 5-7 years. "The production curve for the Appalachian-based wells can go 20-50 years or higher, but the daily volumes from these wells tends to be less than what you might see from a well in …Texas or some parts of Oklahoma."[2] The area you are targeting will have a bearing. Some wells do better, but some do worse. You can extrapolate and guess ahead of time, but the reality is you will never know for sure what the outcome is until the wells are drilled and producing. So, I don't put overriding emphasis on the timing of 'payouts' – but I do take their data, payout time on previous offerings, and the general time frame into consideration and compare it with other offerings. Remember that the goal of your investment is to make money. I do tend to put my emphasis on the sponsor experience and team they have assembled, their track record, their experience in private placement offerings and the fundamentals of the overall program.

What is the estimated cost per well to drill? That is not really possible to answer. There are so many variables involved, including where the drilling is to occur, at what depth (obviously shallow wells are far less costly that deep Gulf waters, for instance) and in what conditions (hard shale, for instance). The geography and conditions will vary; the costs of leasing drilling equipment and buying materials have been going up, and of course if the company owns their equipment the budget is different than leasing. Permit fees and filing fees vary in different states and counties. Insurance is necessary and costly. Subcontractors and teams vary in price. Maybe a road has to be put in to get to the site, and that takes time and money. To give an example, when querying various industry parties: drilling a well for oil and gas in Arizona can cost about one million dollars (a rig capable of drilling holes costs about $15,000 per day *two years ago*); the cost in a deep water expedition can easily be between two million and five million dollars or more; Cotton Valley verticals in eastern Texas are drilled and completed to 8,000 feet at about $1.9-$2 million ($250 per foot); shallow gas and oil in the Appalachian Basin (i.e., 2,000-5,000 feet) are being drilled and completed at cost of about $100 per foot (i.e. up to $500,000). Shallow wells in Illinois may run about $400,000. Drilling horizontal wells in deep, hard deposits such as the Barnett Shale (one of the 'hottest' natural gas plays) can cost about $3 million each or more, compared with $1 million to $1.5 million for a vertical well. Horizontal drilling is costlier because it requires more sophisticated rigs with more powerful motors. Horizontal drilling is the only way to tap formations that otherwise won't give up their gas, and 'fracing' (discussed earlier). In the Woodford Shale, horizontals are reportedly over $5 million (or $555 per foot with multiple-stage slick water frac treatments) with some quotes at $7 million, while the Woodford Shale near Tulsa has shallower depths at 2,700 feet and are reporting estimated costs at $900,000. Brad Updike at Mick & Associates says costs for deeper Marcellus Shale wells drilled in PA vary greatly, with estimates between $1,500,000 up to $4 million.

Why is this topic important? The number of oil and gas scams will rise as the price of oil and gas rises; this can consist of promoters or operators wildly overpricing the cost of wells. Marking up the price of the well 500% to 1,000% gives dubious players absolutely no incentive to produce a viable well. Most offerings that are coming through securities broker-dealers are studied by the Due Diligence departments before they can make their way to the securities representatives you will speak with. The Due Diligence department would not sign off on such a marked-up deal. The reps are usually familiar with oil and gas deals as well, and many tend to recommend trusted and proven sponsors. Offerings that don't pass through the due diligence of a broker dealer have more possibilities of fudging, though some programs are of course very reputable – they just choose not to offer their product through the rigorous and costly Regulation D format. However, programs that might be dubious or have less a chance for success, and those that might solicit directly, need to be looked at even more carefully. Having a general feeling for and knowledge of drilling costs can help arm the educated investor. If an unscrupulous sponsor has marked the program up 500% you will have a feel for this by understanding typical and average drilling costs (and remember, they costs do keep going up!).

Do keep in mind that Regulation D offerings have upfront fees, or load, which normally varies from 12% to 16%.

Some programs are "turn-key" and many are not. Turn-key means that the operator or sponsor knows and has set the budget for the enterprise; if they come in under or at budget (the goal), they keep any of the difference, but if they come in over budget, they pay out of their pockets. Mark up is usually about 10%-18% on turn-key programs.

What the sponsor gets from the program is an important item to review and compare. **"Carried interest"** is often seen in oil and gas deals. What is carried interest? It is a term used by independent oil operators who are selling interests in drilling offering. The operator offers to drill the well if the investors will "carry" or pay his share of the cost. It can be defined as the share of profits from investments made by the investors. Carried interest is most often used by oil companies that have a stake in a property, and in exchange for bringing the deal, the offering and expertise, they receive a portion of the profits or carried interest. Carried interest or "carry", as it is sometimes called, can be said to represent the share of an equity profit for the sponsor. In some cases, the carried interest may transfer to a working interest after the wells are producing. I have seen programs with no carry, but a split of monies in a certain percentage, structured differently but amounting to same thing in the end. Typical carry is 10%-15% but I have also seen 20% and more.

Some programs will have a specific split of profits between the investor and sponsor once cash is flowing from the wells, but no percentage carry. A few programs may pay a 'preferred' return to investors (for instance 10%) before the sponsor takes any profits. They are running the show, they are bringing you the deal and you will rely on their expertise, so they deserve to earn money; but if it is slanted too far to them, or if the plan doesn't seem feasible, then you should look elsewhere. There are plenty of structures, but the bottom line question is: what is the sponsor getting and is it fair, equitable and comparable to other programs?

A **royalty** payment will be part of every deal, made to the landowner(s) where the wells will be drilled. Royalties are paid in exchange for allowing land to be used for drilling (mineral rights), and comes off the top of the sale of the petroleum, before anyone else gets their monies. Royalties are typically 12.5% to 25% of the total revenue on production. If the royalty is greater than 25% it is usually because there is a "carve out" on an overriding interest – ask about it, why it is higher than it should be and where the money is going.

The sponsor may get a specific **Net Revenue Interest**, for instance a percentage of the overall net revenue interest. Net revenue interest is a share of production after all burdens, such as royalties and overriding royalties have been deducted from the working interest. *It is the percentage of production that each party actually receives.* Investors will own a portion of the net revenue income stream (after costs, taxes and royalties are deducted). The **Working Interest**, by the way, is usually defined as portion of the well's costs that an investor is responsible for, usually expressed as a percentage. Working interest is the right to explore, develop and extract the mineral interest granted in the oil and gas lease. The net revenue interest is the percentage of revenues due a working interest owner in a property after deduction of royalties, overriding royalties or other burdens on the property.

There are some offerings where a 'capital call' could be made, especially if one invests as a general partner or a direct working interest. While this rarely occurs with good programs and while there should be a contingency fund set aside, make sure when you are reading your PPM and know what is involved in the offering and what your risk could be.

Some sponsors specialize in more shallow wells in specific areas such as the northeast or Midwest while a larger number of sponsors specialize in mid-depth and deeper wells in Texas and Oklahoma, or the shale plays there (as we discussed in earlier chapters). You will find programs in upstate New York, Pennsylvania, Virginia and the Appalachia's (especially in natural gas), and there are programs in Illinois, Kentucky, Kansas, Colorado, New Mexico as well as Texas and Oklahoma! A few handle the deep Gulf of Mexico deep drilling, which I find more expensive and more risky. There is oil and gas in various places of the U.S. and each has their advantages and disadvantages.

Many sponsors will be sure to target different areas or different fields for diversity. For instance, an offering of 25 wells may include 5 wells in 5 different areas in Texas and Oklahoma (Barnett Shale, Permian Basin, Cotton Valley, Woodford Shale and K-M-A Field) with a combination of oil and gas. To me, a weak offering would be one or a few wells; if they are on the same field, even more risky; if the sponsor is newer or not experienced, even more risky; if they are not capitalized, even riskier; if the structure of the deal doesn't make sense (there is an uneven splitting of profits, or unclear language about the structure in the PPM, or a higher the normal royalty payout or higher carried interest by the sponsor than normal, etc.), then why are you considering it? There are some excellent sponsors and structured programs that make sense; there are a number of average programs, and there are dubious programs.

There may be third-party reports and/or due diligence reports done on the sponsor and the offering by credible third-party due diligence firms, as well as third-party engineering reports. (Some broker-dealers require this as part of the background due diligence before they would agree to sign a selling agreement). Several firms include Synder Kearney and Mick & Associates. In general, the due diligence department of the securities broker-dealer reviews these reports and digs in with their own studies (including background checks of the sponsor and break-down details of the offering). They often conduct a site visit to the sponsor before allowing the offering to be sold by the registered representatives. Brad Updike, with one of the due diligence firms that sees many oil and gas programs believes that because there are so many characteristics and diversity among the programs that good due diligence is especially vital. He says that due diligence red flags to look for are: former litigation, client complaints or regulatory enforcement; older programs with few payouts; limited capitalization; aggressive marketing materials; higher than normal budgets, markups or poor sharing arrangements.

PPMs are not fun to read, as they are full of legal language, risk language and such, but you should read them through and then ask questions. Your rep will assist.

In my own current holdings at this writing, I have a 39 well turn-key offering in a limited partnership format in north and west Texas handled by a local operator; a deepwater Gulf of Mexico offering focusing in natural gas in which the sponsor is teamed up with majors (two wells drilled, a third in progress, five total targeted for the offering); a diversified offering of 26 oil wells, 10 natural gas wells, and another 30 potential re-works, in two areas of Texas and one in New Mexico; an offering of 15 to 20 wells in Oklahoma and Texas (including the Barnett Shale) of about 50% oil and 50% natural gas; and a non-drilling offering whose underlying assets are in the Woodford Shale and whose purpose is high, steady cash flow for three years. I will continue to add a drilling program each year (with something in Appalachia or the middle of the country for added diversity). The cash flows are well above my real estate and general portfolio holdings (and growing) and the tax benefits have been advantageous. Unlike real estate, the offerings have not all been smooth. The deep Gulf drilling had some issues and hit one dry hole; one of the Texas offerings had a slow-down due to a backup of obtaining drilling rigs and teams on the ground. These are the kinds of things that can occur, and an investor must be ready for them and know that the cash flows will not be the same every month…in the case of the deep drilling program, there were some months of no pay at all.

Wells need maintenance – maybe one or two stopped working for a few days before they were fixed and no oil was drawn on those days; companies that pick up the deliveries of oil from the holding tanks may be late and a shipment didn't make it to market as fast; perhaps major storms, floods, hurricanes or tornados created interruptions or delays. There are plenty of things that can happen, small and large, that will affect the day-by-day work and ultimately your cash flow on a monthly basis. You need to understand that if you are going to invest.

Summary Items to Consider before investing in a Drilling Program:

First, always remember to step back and think about your own objectives and if they fit with this investment. Then in summary:

1) **Learn everything you can about the sponsor. Know who you are doing business with!** Your registered representative will help.

2) **Understand what the program objectives are:** where the drilling is to occur – is it in an area of proven reserves and next to producing wells? What kind of drilling conditions are expected in the target areas (which has a bearing on cost, time and outcomes). How are the proven wells doing? What is the expected (conservative) amount of barrels per day in the targeted area, and at what price are the projections based? How do the projected pay-outs compare? What are the direct risks (other than those inherent in any oil and gas deal)? When will drilling begin - must they wait for the offering to be sold out, or will they start earlier?

II. Working Interest / Producing Programs

Investors who would like to see cash flow immediately usually choose a Working interest program in which the drilling has already occurred and the wells are producing. Obviously, the tax benefits from the drilling are not a benefit, but the immediate cash flows can be.

Most of the same comments found in the Drilling section will apply here – the sponsor, the structure, the costs, the sharing of profits, etc. However, the main difference is:

It is important to know the age of the wells you are acquiring as well as their history of production and estimated reserves. What is the general life and performance of the wells in the area and what is the expected life (and depleting rate) of the wells you are acquiring? How are the pressures, and are any reworking of the wells expected?

III. Combination of new drilling and some existing wells.

Some investors like this choice, because they will get some tax write offs (related to how many wells are being drilled and the structure of the offering as to what percentage to expect), and they already have some cash flow for the existing, producing wells. All of the same questions apply as above when reviewing the programs.

IV. Reworks

I have seen only a few pure rework offerings, but I have more often seen reworks in combination with working interests or new drilling. What are 'reworks' and why consider them? Reworking the wells usually means cleaning, flushing or repairing existing well to bring better functionality and production, and hence more income. Sometimes large companies will come in, drill and extract for a while, and then move on to their next find. Smaller companies can pick up these wells and make them more profitable by cleaning and repairing them. Sometimes smaller "mom and pops" have wells but the equipment is in need of repair and they don't have the funds to accomplish this, so the wells are sold. The oil business is a dirty one, and one that requires maintenance! There can be upside for the investor on reworks, but of course it will depend on the overall life of the wells and other factors as discussed earlier. For investors who would like some immediate cash flow and the hope of increasing that flow, reworks included in a program such as drilling could be a supplement.

Review the age and expected life of the wells, and the expectations that reworking the wells will make as far as production and cash flow.

V. Royalty Programs

Royalty programs used to be more common, but the prices to acquire them and to make them work for investor cash flow expectations has become more difficult. There are a few pure royalty programs these days. The typical risks involve the price risk fluctuations of oil and gas, depletion of the wells you are acquiring, and trusting the sponsor.

Royalties are funds received by the land owner from the production of oil or gas, free of costs except taxes. Because royalty programs and some drilling/working interest programs involve land leases (royalty ownership or working interest ownership) or land purchases, considered "like kind" property, these programs are sometimes structured and offered in the 1031 tax-deferred exchanges. Royalty programs can be generally 100% compliant for a tax deferred exchange but drilling or working interests cannot be - you would have some capital gains to pay if you invested 1031 monies into a working interest program. And the programs are not leveraged, which many 1031 investors need in order to fulfill the IRS requirements (meet or beat the amount of debt and equity or pay capital gains). Details are always found in the offering memorandum, and be sure to review the attorney opinion letter.

Note - if you conduct a 1031 exchange from real estate into an oil and gas deal, you will not be able to roll back out into real estate again if the oil and gas deal sells again later (full circle deal) without incurring recapture taxes. If you exchange in, you should expect to stay in oil and gas investments with those funds. Always consult a CPA!

When reviewing a program, look at the projections of production and the price they are basing those projections on. Ask for the engineering reports and data which will show the likely outputs, reserves and success. Royalty programs tend to be more conservative and hold less risk (and less benefits), but I can tell you some royalty investors have been disappointed.

Exit Strategy

Traditionally, when you invest in an oil and gas program, you own those interests until the day the oil or gas runs out and the hole is capped. It depletes. You hopefully gain your return of capital in the initial years and then enjoy cash flow, while diminishing, for some time. However, there are programs now (especially drilling programs) that may have an exit strategy. Always ask, and always refer to the PPM. Some sponsors may intend to sell the offering in 2 to 5 years, as the newly drilled wells will be young enough to still be interesting to buyers. Much will depend on the price of oil and gas, how well the offering has done, the economy and such. Today many institutional buyers (such as insurance companies, pension funds, etc.) are looking for better returns and are buying oil & gas programs. There is never any certainty that your program will be resold, but just having the option to do so can be a benefit.

To end this chapter, I quote John Orban III, who said in his book *"Money in the Ground"*, "If there is a key to successfully investing in oil and gas, it may be as simple as...*participating with good people...who know what they are doing...and who offers a fair deal."*[3] I couldn't agree more!

*As lousy as things are now, tomorrow they will be
somebody's good old days. Gerald Barzan*

*The American consumer each year "seems to know less and care less about
how much energy he or she uses, where it comes from, or what its
true costs are. Americans, it seems, suffer profoundly from what
may soon be known as energy illiteracy; most of us understand
so little about our energy economy that we have no idea that it has
begun to fall apart." Paul Roberts in The End of Oil, 2004.*

"Fraud and falsehood only dread examination. Truth invites it."
Samuel Johnson

CHAPTER 7:
WATCH OUT FOR SCAMS!

The U.S. Postal Service, the Securities and Exchange Commission (SEC), the Texas State Securities Commission and the North American Securities Administrators Association (NASAA) are but four organizations that warn about scams in oil and gas investments.

The U.S. Postal Service tells us that if you are contemplating investing a large amount of money, oil and gas wells may be among the options you are considering. Regardless of what investment opportunities you're considering, it is wise to gather all the information you can so you can make an informed decision.

The Texas Securities Commissioner said in a January 2007 press release, "Securities investments offering profit participation in oil and gas ventures can be legitimate for those who understand and can afford the risk. But too often we are seeing doubtful and even outright fraudulent energy deals aggressively promoted to the public."[1] Ms. Denise Voigt Crawford, the State Commissioner, is also on the Board of Directors with NASAA, and is its President-elect. She says that an investor should do three things before investing: 1) independently research the background of the promoters, 2) get a clear explanation of the deal in writing, and 3) carefully read all the fine print. This matches what we recommend in the previous chapter. She also suggests that an investor contact their own state securities regulator to obtain any public information on the sponsor, since that information might contain red flags. She says, for example, that if the sponsor had a prior conviction for securities fraud, that should give one pause. This matches what we have said about due diligence and essential background checks as well.

The Securities and Exchange Commission (SEC) website mentions some 'red flag warnings' of possible scams. They say that schemes to take advantage of investors abound. Work with a securities broker dealer who can recommend offerings from known sponsors. Due Diligence is important! Some of the 'red flags' are:

1) Use of highly publicized news to lure investors into a 'can't miss' opportunity.

2) Unsolicited materials - ignore junk faxes, emails or voicemails. Most offerings are sold under regulations not allowing solicitation (Regulation D private placements).

3) Pressure selling tactics could be a red flag.

4) Never let a promoter discourage you from talking to your attorney, CPA, or trusted team members. You should be encouraged to consult others.

All of the agencies report that some well deals have been offered by "boiler rooms," or fly-by-night operations that consist of nothing more than bare office space and a dozen or so desks and telephones. The boiler room operators employ telephone solicitors and high-pressure sales tactics. These con artists will make repeated unsolicited telephone calls following scripted pitches and guarantee high profits. (Most oil and gas deals are sold as a security and may be under Regulation D that does not allow solicitation or cold calls, and securities deals can never "guarantee" cash flows or profits.) These scammers say that decisions must be made immediately to get in on the "chance of a lifetime". Beware of unsolicited oil and gas promotions on the internet, by phone, fax and through e-mail.

Ms. Crawford (the Texas Securities Commissioner) cautions the public to the following claims of some scammers: 1) Having an interest in a well "that cannot miss"; 2) that the risks are "minimal" in drilling; 3) that a geologist has given the salesperson "a hot tip"; 4) that there are "tremendous discoveries" nearby; or 5) that "only a few interests remain in this special private deal for a lucky few".

The bottom line: you shouldn't be blindly solicited in these types of offerings in the first place (as we have learned in the chapter about private placements), you should never be pressured, you should know who you are dealing with, you should review and study the offerings, and understand how oil and gas investments work (and the various things that can affect the world of oil and gas) before ever contemplating such an investment.

He who will not economize will have to agonize.
Confucius, Chinese philosopher & reformer (551 BC - 479 BC)

The superior man, when resting in safety, does not forget that danger may
come. When in a state of security he does not forget the possibility of ruin.
When all is orderly, he does not forget that disorder may come. Thus his person
is not endangered, and his States and all their clans are preserved.

Confucius, Chinese philosopher & reformer (551 BC - 479 BC)

CHAPTER 8:
PROS & CONS:
CONCLUSIONS

We have reviewed the "State of Oil and Gas", and understand that use of and reliance on oil and gas is dominant, that we are in an upcoming dire situation but that petroleum use cannot go anywhere soon – and it will most likely become more contentious and difficult as time goes by and supplies slowly deplete. We have reviewed the issues over long-term supply, demand and peak oil. We have touched on the basics of what the oil and gas is and its history, how this commodity works in the market, and some of the factors that affect pricing. We have reviewed the general tax benefits available to investors. We looked at the snapshot reasons why investors choose oil and gas in chapter one, what a direct participation program is, and the general types of investment programs.

Before considering any investment – and I know I have said this several times already - **please remember that energy can be volatile**, more volatile than many types of investments. There are more ups and downs than the typical investment. You have reviewed the issues that can affect pricing, whether political, economic, refinery issues, a rumor or even the weather. An investor who is entirely risk-adverse and who would be worried on a daily basis about the energy industry is probably not made for such an investment. An investor into oil and gas needs to have some risk tolerance and a comfort level in the macro picture, and realize that there will be fluctuations. Investors who are educated about the overall issues on oil and gas, understand the various points made earlier in these chapters, and feel comfortable investing in a desired commodity with tax benefits, may want to proceed. Never ever invest monies into this that you would depend on for living.

Also understand that oil and gas is a **depleting asset**. This is not like real estate whereby you invest in an asset which is bricks and mortar and which should not only maintain its value but appreciate over time. Oil and gas is the opposite. The day drilling begins, the asset will slowly be depleted until it is gone and nothing remains. Typically one invests into the offering, gains the cash flow and tax benefits, hopefully gets a full return on the investment in a handful of years with returns going onward, and essentially owns the interest until the wells runs out. Typical life of an oil well is 20 to 30 years, with declining returns after perhaps 7 to 10 years, depending on location and other factors (this can be longer or shorter). Some sponsors may resell the offering after a few years (I like this potential option); others may not and you will own the deal and collect checks until the oil or gas is gone and no longer producing. Please don't forget the information on Hubbert's Peak and that global oil is declining and depleting.

Potential investors into any oil and gas program should **understand that they are typically paid 60 to 90 days after the oil or gas is pulled from the earth and sold**. It goes through an entire process before the monies make their way back to you. So when prices fluctuate, you don't see the change (either up or down) immediately in the current month's distribution. It is always on a 'look back' basis. Most program sponsors provide very detailed information and reports (or they should) each month to the investors.

You will work with securities broker-dealers and their registered reps who will help you evaluate and choose your investment, while making sure that you fulfill the rules of accreditation and suitability. Your representative should be familiar and knowledgeable about oil and gas deals, and the broker-deal will have a due diligence department that will also review the offering before it is allowed to be sold (including background checks on the sponsor and due diligence details). There is a specific securities license (the Series 22) which is called DPP (direct participation program license). Your rep may have a Series 22, or he may have other licenses that qualify - all the way up to the granddaddy license, the Series 7. It is less important which license your representative has – it is more important that they understand the product, have relationships with good sponsors (issuers or providers of offerings), and that the rep is a fit with you and your style of investing.

You should have at the very least a general understanding of the offering you are considering, but your rep should walk you through and help you understand it more fully, and the program sponsor or engineer should be available to answer questions – your rep will help you with the questions you should be asking! These offerings will always have disclosure documents, key of which is the private placement memorandum (PPM) or offering document. The sponsors and their background, the structure of the deal and proformas, key information about the area and offering will be included. Many sponsors also offer power point education, conference calls, brochures, videos or person-to-person calls to address investment questions.

A few sponsors are reselling the offerings after a 3 to 5 year hold to institutional buyers or others. Buyers are still attracted to the cash flows and diversification, even after the initial more productive years. This option can be good, especially if all principal invested has already been returned or more. Discuss with the sponsor if this is a possibility with their offering or not.

Let's summarize the RISKS or CONS

The cash flow and returns will be based on the price of oil & gas, as well as the supply and demand. While the trends are generally up, this can be affected by politics, economics factors, OPEC decisions, weather, hurricanes or any number of other factors. We have discussed this throughout the book.

The actual price received, or the 'posted price', has become increasingly volatile. The posted prices are influenced by futures prices traded on the NYMEX (New York Mercantile Exchange). So even a rumor about OPEC or a conflict in Iran, for instance, could affect oil prices.

Sponsor risk is a factor. It is important to work with known sponsors who have experience and financial wherewithal, as you don't want to lose your investment due to poor management or a failed company enterprise. Know who you are doing business with. It takes more than high oil and gas prices to make a profit.

Relatively Long-Term and Illiquid. Some oil and gas interests may be individually sold or resold in an auction style situation (depending on the structure), and some offerings may be resold after a certain number of years. However, the investment should be considered relatively illiquid and long-term.

Review Program Structure. There could be risk in the program structure, or if the structure is unfairly weighted towards the sponsor (as in overly high carve-outs on royalties, unfair splits on the back-end, or overly high mark-ups), or if the overall program doesn't seem feasible. Review insurance and other items covered in the program chapter. Be sure there are a number of wells, not just one or several – the risks are higher if that one well or one of a few does not perform. If you have 4 wells and one runs into trouble, 25% of your investment just got into trouble. If your program has many wells and one runs into trouble, there is less impact.

Another risk is of failed wells/dry holes or extremely low pressure /underperformance. That is why we don't normally recommend experimental or wildcatting, where the risk is higher. For the typical investor who wants a drilling program, it is best to stick with developmental drilling handled by an experienced oil company with a track record.

Rising costs. We have learned that a crunch on supplies and people as well as rising costs of the materials needed to extract oil have been growing.

Natural Gas (as opposed to oil) prices are cyclical and depend on the weather. The cold winter months are the high season, but a hurricane could close gas production facilities or even damage or shut them for a time. To offset the differences between oil and gas, consider a program that offers both, or invest in one of each type of program.

Depletion and Decline

Perhaps the largest risk (along with the sponsor risk), and often misunderstood, is the risk of depletion. As we have covered, all wells run dry over some period of time and that after a specific initial period after drilling, there will be varying rates of decline. Unlike with real estate, you won't have a full or even partial value left after a number of years – it will be all gone. This is why a potentially viable and successful program in which you get your return on equity, tax benefits up front and potentially higher cash flow is even more important.

Let's summarize the ADVANTAGES or PROS

Potentially higher cash flows. The cash flow could supplement lower returns from real estate, bonds, funds and many traditional investments. Oil has been hovering above $100 a barrel (at this writing, $142); gas has been continually rising. The potential rewards are advantageous. Most projects would be economically attractive even if oil or gas prices would fall 50%.

An investment can serve as a hedge against the rising prices and oil's impact on various industries, and a hedge against movements on interest rates or stocks.

Tax benefits not available in other investment classes are available with oil and gas. Tax write-offs can also be taken against active, ordinary income while reducing gross income for tax purposes. Investors get accelerated depreciation, and 15% yearly depletion allowances on income they receive from their oil & gas wells until they receive their money back. AMT preference exemption status. The big first year tax write-offs in a drilling program alone can warrant investing in private oil & gas programs for those investors who have yearly incomes exceeding six figures, as long as the program makes sense.

Potential payback in 2 to 5 years. This will obviously vary with the price of petroleum, demand and success of the offering. <u>Returns are not guaranteed, of course</u>. Take time to review programs whereby a number of their programs have paid back. Make sure to study the proformas and projections with your representative.

Better technology. While still risky, the average oil well is less risky than 10 years ago. There is better engineering reports, better technology and better techniques in the field today.

Low Minimums. Program minimums are typically about $25,000 but even $10,000 is possible on some deals. A few require $100,000.

No Leverage. Oil and gas offerings are rarely leveraged.

Diversification of your portfolio.

Who are NOT good candidates for an investment?

Investors must be accredited, of course, which currently means at least one million dollars net worth, or two hundred thousand annual salary (three hundred thousand with a spouse). Investors must be deemed to be suitable as well.

Investors who cannot tolerate any fluctuations or unknowns in an investment, or cannot afford to lose a penny should not invest.

Investors who simply can't get a comfort level or grasp of how oil and gas works.

Investors who may already be quite heavily invested in energy through stocks, funds and such.

Impatient investors – oil and gas, at least in drilling programs, take some time and patience while the sponsor is drilling those wells, and it takes time for the process to make it to the cash flow period (up to a year).

Cash flow does not work like a dividend or a typical real estate cash flow deal – this is an investment into an enterprise, a working interest in most cases (except for royalty programs), and it will have ups and downs and variations depending on a myriad of factors – many of which are out of control of the investor and even the sponsor. There are no guarantees.

Who ARE good candidates for an investment?

An investor who sees the crunch on this commodity and believes prices will stay relatively high, while fluctuating – but can afford the investment if prices fall sharply.

An investor who wants or needs some tax benefits, whether it be write-offs, AMT exclusions or just simple sheltering of the cash flow income.

An investor who wants and needs to diversify their portfolio.

An investor who has gotten a comfort level with this asset-type and at least a basic understanding of it.

An investor who doesn't need liquidity with the funds invested.

Obviously, an accredited and suitable investor!

An investor who can see the potential – perhaps as some have said, into one of the greatest investment events of the century.

I realize that oil and gas investments are not made for everyone. For the investor who fulfils the above criteria and who has really worked to understand and get comfortable with the elements and facts involved,

I think there can be great opportunity. As Peter Tertzakian said, "In fact, our problems aren't going to go away for a decade or more. North American addiction to cheap energy is too strong, and the technological standards of the last century too entrenched, for any new or different approach."[1] The writing is on the wall, and high prices and struggles with oil and gas are head of us, even as breakthrough alternatives start to make their way in. **We are going to struggle as consumers, but we can offset some of that through smart investments.**

"Our ignorance is not so vast as our failure to use what we know."
M. King Hubbert
(from Energy and Power, A Scientific American Book, 1971)

"Oil Warrior: This man ran the CIA, fought the Cold War, and averted
nuclear Armageddon. Now he says that if you want to beat BinLaden, buy a
Prius."
Story about James Woolsey at Motortrend.com

Those who are unwilling to invest in the future haven't earned one.
H.W. Lewis, Technological Risk, 1990

Foul cankering rust the hidden treasure frets,
But gold that's put to use more gold begets.
William Shakespeare, "Venus and Adonis" 1593

CHAPTER 9:
CLOSING COMMENTS

I believe, as stated earlier, that we are in a pivotal era regarding oil and gas. It is easy to envision that the energy world and therefore the world in general will have nasty shakeups in the next decades because of struggles over oil, and also that new technologies and alternatives will need to be in the picture fast. We have to realize oil won't be here forever, that prices will probably remain relatively high though volatile, and that the world's larger reserves are controlled outside our borders, which makes us more vulnerable. The U.S. only has 2% of the world's total reserves.

Our thriving economy and that of the world is based on oil and the threat of its impending loss is almost too heavy to imagine. The ideal world would be one in which a number of alternative energies make their way forward – hopefully cleaner, renewable ones for better overall impact on the world to work in concert with oil and gas. I can see solar and wind making great strides, better hybrids or especially electric cars being used by the population in general in the next decade, and cleaner electricity being generated. But will a combination of all of the alternatives be strong enough and will there be enough development at this late stage for the potential crisis ahead? Will enough people get it, pay attention and demand that we work together for a common goal;

will researchers have enough support to take the necessary technologies to the next step; and will politicians be courageous enough to act?

So as stated before, all of the current elements at play over oil and gas seems to make it a **timely investment**, as we have learned in the book. **Cash flows** are typically higher on these investments than in many other investments – but are not guaranteed and will always be somewhat volatile; **tax benefits** are exceptional on drilling programs; payouts (return on capital) could be seen within five years on good drilling offerings – but are not guaranteed of course, and will vary with the program structure as we have learned in the book. Oil and gas investments can hedge against inflation and against moves on the stock market and help your portfolio.

My two closing comments can be summarized as:

1) **Wake up and investigate for yourself** this tremendously dire situation we are heading for and get proactive about it on any level you can, even if it is just personal conservation, support of alternatives and talking to your political representatives. (I can't wait to get an electric car or hybrid when my current lease runs out at the end of 2009; the house we are currently building is incorporating solar and other new exciting technologies).

2) **Take a prudent look at oil and gas investments NOW.**

Oil and gas has and will have still a primary place in our lives for some time to come. With my "investor hat" on, I am not missing out on the oil and gas opportunities, and I hope that you won't either! Just be careful and make reasoned decisions about the sponsors and their proposed programs using the guidelines here and from other experts.

FOOTNOTES

Chapter 1.
1. CBC News Online. "*Supply and Demand: World oil markets under pressure.*" April 28, 2005.
2. Associated Press release. May 22, 2008.
3. Sandalow, David. *Freedom from Oil.* (McGraw Hill Publishers). Page 3
4. Cambridge Energy Research Associates (CERA) website.
5. PIMCO website.
6. Samuelson, Robert. Washington Post editorial "*Shoot the Speculators!*". July 2, 2008.
7. CERA website.
8. Sandalow, David. Freedom from Oil (McGraw Hill Publishers).
9. Weidner, William E. *Oil & Gas Investor.* January 31, 2003.

Chapter 2
1. Needham, Paul. Yale Daily News. "*Forum tackles issues of law, energy*". November 12, 2007.
2. Hicks, Brian and Nelder, Chris. *Profit from the Peak.* (John Wiley & Sons) pg 5.
3. Bartlett, Roscoe. Interviewed in the film "A Crude Awakening", 2006. Directed and produced by Basil Gelpke and Ray McCormack.
4. Savinar, Matthew David. Inverviewed in the film "A Crude Awakening", 2006. Directed and produced by Basil Gelpke and Ray McCormack.
5. Tertzakian, Peter. *A Thousand Barrels A Second.* (McGraw Hill Publishers)
6. OECD. World Energy Outlook 2007.
7. Hard Assets Investor website. "*Energy Markets*". November 2007.
8. Brush, Michael. MSN Money website. "*It's time to invest for $100 oil*". September 2006.

9. Batson, Andrew and King, Neil Jr. Wall Street Journal. *"China Lifts Fuel Prices, and Oil Falls in Response"*. June 20, 2008.

10. St. Petersburg Times, *"Nigerian Oil Facility Raided"*. June 20, 2008.

11. Wall Street Journal. June 21, 2008.

12. Mouawad, Jad. New York Times. July 22, 2007.

13. The Washington Post. August 2, 2007.

14. American Petroleum Institute website.

15. Investor's Business Daily, Letter to the editor by Chris Nelder. July 9, 2008.

16. King, Neil Jr. Wall Street Journal. *"Global Oil Supply Worries Fuel Debate in Saudi Arabia – Former Officials at Odds over "Peak" Theory; Crude Hits High"*. June 27, 2008.

17. Hicks, Brian and Nelder, Chris. *Profit from the Peak*. (John Wiley & Sons).

18. Hicks, Brian and Nelder, Chris. *Profit from the Peak*. (John Wiley & Sons)

19. "The World's Giant Oil Fields" by Matthew Simmons, 2002; as noted in *Profit from the Peak*.

20. Nelder, Chris. Newletter, Energy and Capital. "The Truth About Oil". 2008.

21. Roberts, Paul. *The End of Oil*. 2004 (Houghton Mifflin)

22. Mufson, Steven. Washington Post. *"Oil Price Rise Causes Global Shift in Wealth"*. November 10, 2007.

23. Wall Street Journal. November 19, 2007.

24. Study by Rembrandt Koppelaar, ASPO-Netherlands.

25. Hicks, Brian and Nelder, Chris. *Profit from the Peak*. (John Wiley & Sons).

26. Investor's Business Daily, Letter to the editor by Chris Nelder. July 9, 2008

27. Hamilton, James. "Oil shale hits a freeze". Econbrowser.com. June 17, 2007.

28. Independent Petroleum Association of America website.

29. Investor's Business Daily, Letter to the editor by Chris Nelder. July 9, 2008

30. Tertzakian, Peter. *A Thousand Barrels A Second*. (McGraw Hill Publishers)

31. CBC News Online. *"Supply and Demand: World oil markets under pressure."* April 28, 2005

32. ASPO press release by Mikael Hook. "OPEC: Oil prices won't come down". June 24, 2008.

33. Hirsch, Robert; Bezdek, Roger; Wendling, Robert. "The Hirsch Report." February 2005.

34. Council on Foreign Relations report, "National Security Consequences of U.S. Oil Dependency". 2006.

35. Reed, Stanley. Businessweek. "An Inconvenient Trust About Oil". Dec 31, 2007

36. CERA. "Dawn of a New Age: Global Energy Scenarios for Strategic Decision-Making –The Energy Future to 2030." 2006.

37. Yergin, Daniel. The Financial Times. May 28, 2008.

38. Salopek, Paul. *"The Pay Zone"*. Chicago Tribune. July 29, 2006

39. Bary, Andrew. Barrons. *"Bountiful Barrels: Where to Find $140 Trillion)*.

40. Mulson, Steven. Washington Post. "Oil Price Rise Causes Global Shift in Wealth." November 10, 2007.

41. Mulson, Steven. Washington Post. "Oil Price Rise Causes Global Shift in Wealth." November 10, 2007

42. Pilkington, Ed. The Guardian. "Big oil to big wind: Texas veteran sets up $10B clean energy project". Monday April 14, 2008

43. St. Petersburg Times. "FPL Goal: 3 Solar Plants in 2009". June 26, 2008.

44. Mulson, Steven. Washington Post. "Oil Price Rise Causes Global Shift in Wealth." November 10, 2007

45. Frillici, Leigh. Houston 11 News. "Ethanol fuel may be harming your vehicle." May 27, 2008.

46. "The Many Problems with Ethanol from Corn: Just How Unsustainable Is It?" Joint report by *Professor Tadeusz Patzek, A Professor of Chemical Engineering University of California at Berkeley , Professor David Pimentel Department of Agricultural*

Science Cornell University Michael Wang, Christopher Saricks and May Wu Authors of the Argonne National Laboratory Report "Fuel-Cycle Fossil Energy Use and Greenhouse Gas Emissions of Fuel Ethanol Produced from the U.S. Midwestern Corn" Hosein Shapouri, James Duffield and Michael Wang Authors of the USDA Report: The Energy Balance of Corn Ethanol

47. San Diego Union Tribune. "*Fuel's Gold: Turning Corn into Ethanol May not be Worth It*". August 3, 2005.

48. Food and Agriculture Organization of the United Nations (FAO), website.

49. Marinis, Alexandre. "*U.S. Ethanol isn't up to Brazilian Smackdown*". Bloomberg. May 27, 2008.

50. Hicks, Brian and Nelder, Chris. *Profit from the Peak*. (John Wiley & Sons).

51. Wolfe, Josh. Forbes Magazine. "*Breakthrough Technologies For 2008*". January 17, 2008.

52. Buss, Dale. Fully Charged Journal. "For highway-safe electric vehicles, the long wait is almost over – really!" May 8, 2007.

53. Linton, Lascelle. Toronto Star. "Electric Car that recharges its battery with only regenerative breaking?" Feb 4, 2008.

54. Hicks, Brian and Nelder, Chris. *Profit from the Peak*. (John Wiley & Sons).

55. Agassi, Shai. Panel discussions at The Brookings Institute conference, "Plug In Electric Vehicles 2008: What role for Washington". June 11-12,2008.

56. Kunstler, James Howard. The Long Emergency. (Grove Press)

57. Leeb, Stephen and Leeb, Donna. *The Oil Factor*. (Warner Business Books)

58. Roberts, Paul. *The End of Oil*. 2004 (Houghton Mifflin)

59. Tertzakian, Peter. *A Thousand Barrels A Second*. (McGraw Hill Publishers)

60. Hicks, Brian and Nelder, Chris. *Profit from the Peak*. (John Wiley & Sons).

61. Tertzakian, Peter. *A Thousand Barrels A Second*. (McGraw Hill Publishers)

62. Oliver, Rachel. CNN.com "All About Food & Fossil Fuels". March 17, 2008.

63. Orban, John III. *Let's Talk An Oil Deal.* (Meridien Press).
1991.

Chapter 3
History section drawn from Business and Economics Research
Advisor (BERA) with thanks.
1. Campbell, Colin. "Understanding Peak Oil", ASPO website.
2. Orban, John III. *Money in the Ground.* (Meridien Press).
2006.
3. Tertzakian, Peter. *A Thousand Barrels A Second.* (McGraw Hill
Publishers)
4. Nelder, Chris. Newletter, Energy and Capital. "*The Truth
About Oil*".
5. King, Neil Jr. Wall Street Journal. "*Cries in the Dark*". June
30, 2008.
6. CERA. "Dawn of a New Age: Global Energy Scenarios for
Strategic Decision-Making –The Energy Future to 2030."
2006
7. American Petroleum Institute website.
8. Powerline News website. May 23, 2008.
9. Charlie Rose television show.
10. Roberts, Paul. *The End of Oil.* 2004 (Houghton Mifflin)

Chapter 4
1. The International Crude Oil Market Handbook, 2004.
2. Samuelson, Robert. Washington Post editorial "*Shoot the
Speculators!*." July 2, 2008.
3. Airhart, Marc. "The Father of the Barnett Shale". Geology.
com.
4. Shottenkirk, Jerry. KFOR.com. "*Technology changes lift the
Woodford Shale*". March 26, 2007.
5. Casselman, Ben. Wall Street Journal. July 18, 2008
"*Continental Shift: BP is the Latest Gas Player*".
6. Brian and Nelder, Chris. *Profit from the Peak.* (John Wiley &
Sons).

7. Hicks, Brian and Nelder, Chris. *Profit from the Peak*. (John Wiley & Sons) pg 101.
8. Weeks, Jennifer. The Environment Magazine. "Highly combustible: debating the risks and benefits of LNG." Nov-Dec 2005.
9. Loder, A. St. Peterburg Times. *"Fuel costs, power bills rise together"*. June 29, 2008.
10. BERA

Chapter 5
1. In the case of Gregory v. Helvering 69 F.2d 809, 810 (2d Cir. 1934), aff'd, 293 U.S. 465, 55 S.Ct. 266, 79 L.Ed. 596 (1935)
2. United States Oil and Gas Corporation website
3. Hennessee, Patrick and Hennessee, Sean, editors. *Oil and Gas, Federal Income Taxation 2007 edition*. CCH, a Wolters Kluwer business.

Chapter 6
1. Brown, Thomas E. *Layman's Guide to Oil and Gas Investments*. (Gulf Publishing) 1981.
2. Updike, Brad, Mick & Associates. "Energy Update Newsletter May 2008".
3. Orban, John III. *Money in the Ground*. (Meridien Press). 2006

Chapter 7
1. Crawford, Denise Voigt (Texas State Commissioner). 2007 Press Release, Texas State Board of Securities.

Chapter 8
1. Tertzakian, Peter. *A Thousand Barrels A Second*. (McGraw Hill Publishers).

SUGGESTED READING

Books:

Hicks, Brian and Nelder, Chris. *Profit from the Peak; the end of oil and the greatest investment event of the century.* John Wiley & Sons. 2008.

Leeb, Stephen and Leeb, Donna. *The Oil Factor.* Warner Business Books. 2004.

Tertzakian, Peter. *A Thousand Barrels A Second.* McGraw-Hill. 2007.

Kunstler, James Howard. *The Long Emergency.* Grove Press. 2005.

Orban, John, III. *Money in the Ground.* Meridien Press. 4th edition 2006.

Deffeyes, Kenneth. *Hubbert's Peak: the impending world oil shortage.* 2001. Princeton University Press.

Thompson, Stephen. *Your American Birthright: Investing in Oil and Gas.* New Renaissance Publishing. 2007.

Roberts, Paul. *The End of Oil.* Houghton Mifflin. 2004.

Sandalow, David. *Freedom From Oil.* McGraw Hill. 2008.

Heinberg, Richard. *The Party's Over. Oil War and the Fate of Industrial Societies.* New Society Publishers. 2003.

Heinberg, Richard. *PowerDown. Options and actions for a post-carbon world.* New Society Publishers. 2004.

Hennessee, Patrick and Sean. *Oil and Gas Federal Income Taxation 2007.* CCH, a Wolters Kluwer business. 2006.

Yergin, Daniel. *The Prize*. Free Press. 1991.

Simmons, Matthew R. Twilight *in the Desert. The coming Saudi oil shock and the world economy.* John Wiley & Sons. 2005.

Newsletters:
WTRG Economist has a frequent newsletter that is strong on data, statistics and depth on the oil & gas industry. James Williams is the author and has been in the industry for decades and is extremely knowledgable. www.wtrg.com for the link.

EV World newsletter.

Films on DVD:
Who Killed the Electric Car? Documentary film by Chris Paine. Sony Pictures Classic. 2006.

A Crude Awakening. Documentary film directed and produced by Basil Gelpke, Ray McCormack. 2006. Lava Productions AG, Zurich. Winner of the Zurich Filmprize.

Breinigsville, PA USA
15 February 2011
255637BV00001B/50/P

[9]